Get Your

ASSETS to Work

4 Steps to Build Generational Wealth

By:

Curtis D. Haines

Stop trading time for money.

"Get your assets to work so you don't have to." –Curtis Haines.

Vende Cap Publishing

Disclaimer Notice:

Please note the information contained within this book is for educational and entertainment purposes only. All effort has been executed to present accurate, up-to-date, and reliable, complete information. No warranties of any kind are declared or implied. Readers acknowledge that the author does not render legal, financial, medical, or professional advice. The content within this book has been derived from various sources. Please consult a licensed professional before attempting any techniques outlined in this book.

By reading this document, the reader agrees that under no circumstances is the author responsible for any losses, direct or indirect, which are incurred as a result of the use of the information contained within this book, including, but not limited to, – errors, omissions, or inaccuracies.

ISBN: 979-8-9888615-0-8

Library of Congress Control Number: 2023916027

Contents

Foreword

By Del Walmsley, Founder and President of Lifestyles Unlimited Inc.

In 1990, after two-and-a-half years of investing in real estate, I retired at 34 years of age. At the time, I very quickly realized that what I accomplished was not only exciting but also quite uncommon. I found myself with a lot of free time and no friends to spend it with. That's when I started studying wealth and wealth production and attending seminars on the subject. I attended seminar after seminar only to find that they all fell into two kinds: boring, repetitive presentations on why I and others should put our money in traditional investments like 401k, IRA, stocks, bonds, etc., *and* crazy something for nothing, midnight madness, seminars making claims that their system would make you rich overnight.

I decided there needed to be a practical, real-world training program that would teach people how I had used real estate to retire in such a short time. At the time, I had no idea that this would lead to the largest real estate investment training program in the world. Teaching and mentoring people from all over the country, from all classes of people, I found many very intelligent, highly educated people who just couldn't get the types of financial results they wanted using the business models they were using. Once they got their hands on the correct business model, they were able to create millions of dollars in profits in very short periods of time.

Curtis Haines caught my attention right away. His attention to detail and advanced understanding of business, accounting, and sales were a powerful combination of skills that set him aside in my mind right away. It didn't take long to see him take what I was teaching and start adding his own ideas that extended the effectiveness of the system. At the same time, he and some of his friends started meeting in a small group to share their ideas to exponentially expand both the rate and range of financial growth they could produce using the system. I started using these new ideas and teaching them to the rest of my members. This new upgraded level of education created an explosion of wealth production in the group.

Today, Lifestyles Unlimited Inc. is available to students anywhere in the world. We have members in all 50 states and many other countries. I asked Curtis to come on board as a mentor and teach his great ideas to benefit thousands, and he agreed. While teaching, he found, as I did, that the more people you help, the more deals you are involved with, the better you get at it, and the more money you make yourself. To my surprise, Curtis continued to grow his wealth to a level higher than all my other students. He was the first Lifestyles member to own over a **Billion Dollars** in real estate! This made him the natural person for me to spend hours with discussing how to manage large amounts of the family's money for the future. We both saw that there is little to no education out there for wealthy people who now must control their family's wealth from one generation to the next. Curtis once again took it upon himself to do deep research into this topic and report back with the information. He concluded that the material was not in an organized, easy-to-follow format. This is his first book, sharing the ideas he has been teaching to our members for years. As is everything Curtis does, it is great.

If you want to learn how to build wealth and how very wealthy people grow their wealth across many generations, you **MUST** read this book. I am very proud to know Curtis, and I am sure this book will help tens of thousands of people change their financial lives.

Chapter 1

Introduction

Fifteen years ago, my life took an unexpected turn when I was forced to sell my company and start over. This sudden change in direction left me feeling like I had lost a part of myself. The employees were more than just colleagues; they were my second family. It was a devastating experience, leaving me unsure of my next steps. Thankfully, a good friend introduced me to the world of multifamily real estate. Real estate became my beacon of hope. Real estate was this new opportunity that helped ease the pain of losing my company and my entire support system.

The plan was simple: purchase an apartment complex that would generate enough cash flow to match my previous income. With the help of my mentor, I found a 176-unit apartment that perfectly aligned with my goals, and without hesitation, I signed the purchase contract. With a 90-day timeline to close the deal, everything seemed to be falling into place. Property inspections went smoothly, and the lender approved our loan, signaling the beginning of the closing process.

As stipulated in the purchase contract, I initiated the wire transfer to cover the remaining half of the required earnest money deposit. The next day, the title company notified me that my funds had not arrived. I called my bank, and they were just as surprised as me. The bank initiated the wire again, but the funds never arrived.

Unknown to me, all my money from the sale of my previous business had been deposited into a mutual fund heavily invested in Lehman Brothers' bonds. The collapse of Lehman Brothers in 2008 sent shockwaves throughout the financial markets, and within a matter of days, all my hard-earned funds vanished.

I didn't go to Vegas and gamble my money away. I didn't blow my money on a big mansion and expensive cars like most lottery winners seem to do. I wasn't doing anything high-risk, like trying to short the next high-flying stock. All I did was deposit my money in a mutual fund held in one of the country's largest and most respected brokerage firms. They assured me my funds were well protected by additional insurance coverages beyond FDIC and SIPC limits. Unfortunately, there is no protection for a complete market collapse.

In an instant, my beacon of hope crumbled. The pain from the forced sale of my previous business and the loss of my funds overwhelmed me. The next six months were extremely difficult. I was days away from transferring my funds to escrow and closing on my first property. Days away from securing my family's future. I was depressed, and I almost gave up on real estate.

It is easy to look back and say this setback turned out to be a blessing in disguise. But like most life events, it's hard to see anything when you are at rock bottom. Thankfully, I had the support of an amazing community of like-minded real estate investors who were willing to lend a helping hand to pull me out of that dark hole of despair. Losing all of my money forced me to change my business plan completely and venture in an entirely different direction.

Fortunately, I stayed in real estate and hit my original financial goal on my third acquisition. I was pleasantly surprised by my level of determination and how fast things improved. I had no backup plan, so I had to make it work. What helped me the most was seeing other people take the first few steps towards uncertainty and succeed. My first two properties were purchased in 2009, and I closed on my third property in early 2011.

People often ask me why I didn't stop there. If you were financially independent at that point in time, why keep working harder and harder to buy more and more properties? The truth is, I was having way too much fun. It didn't feel like work. And somewhere around my fifth or sixth acquisition, I noticed it was getting easier. With growth came the full benefits of economies of scale. I worked less and enjoyed it more. As my portfolio expanded, I had a team of dedicated individuals to take on tasks that were once solely mine. Everything just became progressively smoother—better opportunities, bigger deals, more off-market deals, and a faster accumulation of income-producing assets.

Around my 20th acquisition, I met high-net-worth families with different perspectives on business and investing. And around my 30th acquisition, I experienced another illuminating "ah-ha" moment that made me reevaluate my business model.

One of my long-time investors, who had been investing with me since the beginning, introduced me to a friend. Someone that his family has known for many, many years. This individual turned out to be a third-generation member of a very wealthy family, overseeing their finances through their family office. Discovering the concept of a family office and seeing how they approached business and investing forever changed my real estate trajectory. In this book, I will share my story and the invaluable lessons I've learned. By the time you reach the end, I hope you will adopt a similar mindset, empowering you to build real wealth for your family and future generations.

You see, high-net-worth families have a specific strategy you can duplicate. Their strategy will help guide you through all of your investing decisions and help filter through the plethora of information you need to learn in real estate. This strategy inspired me to take my investing to a whole new level. Over the past 15 years, I have been involved in 187 real estate acquisitions and 63 real estate dispositions valued in excess of $4.4 billion. A total of 32,335 apartment units spread across 187 apartment communities. The majority of my assets were acquired within the last five years using this strategy.

In the pages that follow, I invite you to embark on a journey—one that merges my personal experiences, wisdom gained from high-net-worth families, and a tried-and-true approach to real estate investing. Together, we will explore the depths of this strategy, empowering you to create a lasting legacy of wealth for yourself and your family.

Welcome to a new world of possibilities.

Chapter 2

The Beginning of My Real Estate Journey

I was introduced to real estate by a close friend, a highly accomplished business owner in the staffing industry. For over ten years, we would regularly talk on the phone, sharing stories about our respective businesses and anything related to staffing and recruiting. Her flourishing growth was evident; she continuously expanded her company by opening new offices and exploring specialized areas within the recruiting industry.

However, one day, she surprised me with her sudden decision to sell her company and transition into real estate. I could not fathom why she would leave behind such a successful venture for the uncertainties of the real estate world. At that time, my understanding of real estate was limited to what I had seen on television—people buying dilapidated houses, demolishing walls and cabinets, and transforming them into beautiful living spaces.

We lost touch after she ventured into real estate. I was distracted by the rapid growth of my staffing company. I didn't know she joined a real estate education and mentoring group called Lifestyles Unlimited. This group helped thousands of families achieve financial independence through investments in single-family and multifamily properties.

Fast forward two years—at this point, our roles had reversed. I found myself confiding in her about my own struggles following the unexpected sale of my staffing business without a clear plan for the future. I always admired her business savvy in the staffing industry and was confident she could help me figure out my next move. Although I had a few business ideas in mind, I was surprised when she suggested that I explore the world of real estate, just as she had done.

Initially, I dismissed the idea, as I could not picture myself wielding a sledgehammer and tearing down walls. She swiftly corrected my misconceptions by explaining her involvement in the apartment industry and drawing comparisons to the staffing industry, allowing me to grasp the business aspect. It wasn't just real estate —it was a business that involved real estate.

Eye of The Hurricane

Her explanation and elaboration of the idea sparked a fire within me, compelling me to join Lifestyles Unlimited without hesitation. Little did I know, diving into this world felt like attempting to drink from an open fire hydrant—an overwhelming flood of information engulfed me. Nevertheless, the odds were on my side as the individuals I met at Lifestyles were eager to assist. They guided me through the entire process, gradually instilling the confidence and knowledge required for this new venture into multifamily real estate.

Based on the feedback from my mentor, becoming an independent rental owner—an individual property owner—seemed to be the most fitting path for me. The other options within multifamily real estate involved partnerships, but given my negative experience with a previous partnership, I was not keen on forming another one. In a previous business endeavor, I had started a staffing company with two other partners. We were forced to sell the company because of partner related issues. Considering all these factors, becoming an independent rental owner appeared to be my ideal choice.

When I joined Lifestyles Unlimited in May 2008, the organization's founder and primary mentor, Del Walmsley, had reduced his real estate purchasing activities. By then, he had already amassed an impressive real estate portfolio and had dedicated most of his time to assisting other members in acquiring real estate. However, after the financial collapse of 2008, he reemerged as an active buyer. It is worth noting that most of the world was not investing in real estate during that period. The 2008 collapse drastically altered the lending and real estate landscapes. Yet, like a lone voice in the wilderness, Del Walmsley passionately encouraged his members to seize this once-in-a-lifetime buying opportunity. His energy and enthusiasm were unparalleled, reminiscent of a child set loose in a candy store.

As I mentioned earlier, I lost all my money due to the Lehman Brothers bankruptcy, which occurred just days before I was set to close on my first apartment acquisition. Devastated and unsure of my next move, I found myself caught between Del's message of this being a once-in-a-lifetime buying opportunity and the harsh reality of my financial situation. Seeking guidance, I turned to Del, expressing my predicament. He sternly looked me in the eye and simply said, "Figure it out. Find a way." Those words resonated deeply within me, and a few months later, with the assistance of Lifestyles Unlimited, I stumbled upon the perfect property listed at a significant discount.

Leap of Faith

Del's contagious excitement, boundless energy, and unwavering conviction convinced me I had to find a way. I started believing there was a way, even if I could not see it at the moment. Despite having no available funds, I decided to venture into partnerships. Examining my monthly brokerage statements, I noticed that the mutual fund responsible for my financial loss still had a net asset value (NAV) of 1, indicating some residual value.

Drawing inspiration from Del's earlier days in real estate, during which he bought numerous single-family homes using his credit cards, I pondered a similar approach. Could I borrow against the margin funds in my brokerage account to achieve a similar feat?

Taking a leap of faith, I wrote a substantial check to myself, deposited it into my checking account, and to my surprise, it cleared successfully. I couldn't believe it. The funds were gone, but they were willing to loan me money on margin as if the funds were still there.

Suddenly, I had the money necessary to pursue the partnership opportunity. Following Del's guidance, I formed a partnership with 15 other families, pooling our resources to acquire the property. In early 2009, we completed the transaction, and technically, I purchased my first apartment using personal credit.

I am incredibly grateful to the 15 families who gave me their trust and invested in my first property. Being new to this, I had doubts about my ability to raise such a large amount of money in a short period, especially with the current economic challenges.

Six months later, fueled by the success of my initial investment, I established another partnership and acquired my second apartment using credit from my margin account.

Although I wasn't actively searching at the time, fate intervened when I received a call from the same real estate broker who had facilitated my first purchase. To my surprise, the property was located just a block away, under the ownership of the same real estate investment trust (REIT) that sold me my first property.

When I acquired my first property from this REIT, I was an unknown buyer with no real estate experience. I remember our first conference call where they would decide whether or not to award me the sales contract. We had already agreed on the price and terms, but they wanted to confirm that I was a legitimate buyer who could close on time. I spent days preparing for the call because I knew they would go with another buyer if I didn't sound confident and knowledgeable. By the time the conference call started, I was ready. I had memorized my business plan and their financials, and I even studied previous buyer questionnaires to be prepared for tough questions. I practiced my Q&A with anyone who would listen and was ready to impress them.

I joined the conference call and found that most participants were already chatting about personal matters. I recognized my team members but couldn't distinguish the voices of the seller's team. My team included my real estate broker, mortgage broker, and real estate attorney, while the seller's team consisted of the listing broker, owner, and their real estate attorney.

After a brief exchange of pleasantries, the listing broker suggested we introduce ourselves. I can't recall the exact order of introductions, but when it was my attorney's turn, the call ended quickly and in a surprisingly positive way. It turned out that my attorney and the owner's attorney were good friends, and everyone on the call already knew each other. When the owner learned who was on my team, he simply suggested moving forward with signing the contract without any further questions.

My jaw dropped. The owner didn't ask me a single question. I said nothing other than a quick introduction. I experienced firsthand the importance of building relationships in business transactions. People want to do business with people they know and trust. Having one or two key members on your team who are well-known and respected can help bridge that gap.

The second acquisition from the same REIT was easy. They already knew who was on my team, and our first acquisition closed on time without any issues. We used the same sales contract from our first acquisition, made a few minor updates, and both parties quickly signed the contract. With the assistance of the same lender, our second transaction smoothly closed over the Christmas holidays.

Eighteen months later, I unexpectedly received half of my lost funds from the Lehman Brothers bankruptcy, enabling me to pay off both margin loans. This turn of events surprised me, as previous legal notices had indicated little to no recovery. With the remaining funds, I purchased my third and fourth apartments. To fill any remaining gaps, we formed two more partnerships. All four properties were conveniently located within walking distance of each other in one of Houston's most robust rental markets.

We acquired the third property out of foreclosure, and it had been in receivership for a couple of years. The roofs were still covered with blue tarps, which were a result of the damages caused by Hurricane Ike in 2008. Occupancy was low, and the property required substantial repairs. This was a textbook "value add" that ended up exceeding our expectations. The closing process was quite challenging due to the limited documentation provided by the seller and the low occupancy. Our success with the previous two properties helped us persuade the lender that we could turn this property around.

The fourth property was another unique acquisition. I got a phone call from the seller's broker asking me if I could close in 60 days. The owner was on the verge of losing the property if it wasn't closed within 60 days from the day I received the call. At that time, closing took 90 days from the signed contract - 30 days for buyer inspections and 60 days for the lender to close.

As a seasoned salesperson with 14 years of experience, I knew that saying no would mean the seller's broker would call someone else. So, I confidently said yes and asked for the contract to be sent right away. I immediately consulted my mentor, who provided me with the necessary guidance to close the deal in record time. We successfully closed on the 59th day, making it the most stressful acquisition to date.

Although I have closed deals in less than 60 days from the signed purchase contract, this remains the only one I have closed within 60 days from the first call.

A big thank you to Shelley, Brandon, Keith, Russell, and Cliff for helping me with my first four acquisitions and laying the foundation to buy more.

Over the next few years, I acquired five more properties in the same submarket, expanding our Galleria portfolio to 1,977 units spread across nine apartment communities. Along the same timeline, I added five more properties to another thriving rental market in Houston, growing our Sugar Land portfolio to 844 apartment units. Location and economies of scale played a pivotal role in our success.

Despite my initial success in real estate, a chance encounter introduced me to the power of an entire business focused on maximizing assets. Inspired, I started my family office and adopted their 30-day rule for deploying funds. This sense of urgency propelled my wealth accumulation, and I achieved billion-dollar milestones in record time. By shifting my mindset and following four key steps—replacing non-income-producing assets with income-producing assets, using leverage, capturing equity gains early, and maximizing return on net worth—I experienced exponential growth. In the next chapter, I will share my transformative experience with the family office concept of building wealth.

Chapter 3

Introduction to A Family Office

Just before my encounter with a family office, I was thriving. I had a strong portfolio of properties concentrated in two main locations. Additionally, I had ventured into new cities beyond Houston and even outside of Texas. The strategic execution of cash-out refinances and property sales substantially increased my cash reserves. The monthly cash flow generated from my properties exceeded even my most optimistic projections.

The Meeting

My calendar was always packed with daily property visits and various business meetings. Throughout the years, I have had numerous meetings with potential investors or individuals seeking real estate advice. I always enjoyed these one-on-one interactions. So, when one of my investors introduced me to a good friend of his family, I assumed it would be another typical meeting. Little did I know that this meeting would profoundly impact my real estate business.

I was immediately impressed by the upscale modern decor when I entered his office. Curious, I asked him about his line of work and if this was his corporate office. To my surprise, he responded, "No, this is my family office. I spend most of my time investing."

In an attempt to hide my ignorance, I casually replied, "Oh, okay," pretending to understand what he meant fully. I knew the meaning of "family business," but I had never heard someone say "family office." We spent the rest of the meeting discussing real estate. He was asking a lot of good questions. Unfortunately, time flew by, and our meeting ended before I could delve into his background. Afterward, I wasted no time in Googling "family office," and the search results enlightened me:

> *A family office is a business entity solely dedicated to maximizing the return on a specific family's assets. It operates under the guidance of a CEO, CFO, and a supporting team, all working towards this common objective.*

While I believed I was already doing a good job maximizing my assets, the idea of having an entire business focused on this endeavor astounded me. Starting a family office required a minimum net worth of $1 billion back then. Admittedly, I fell short of that mark by a few zeros.

Nonetheless, embracing the motto "fake it until you make it," I established my own family office, naming myself the CEO of Haines Family Office LLC.

> *"Don't let a good life get in the way of a great life."*
> *–Del Walmsley.*

The 30-Day Rule

Engaging in further research and learning more about my wealthy acquaintance, I discovered their 30-day rule. Whenever a substantial sum of funds returned to the family office, the team had 30 days to reinvest it. As CEO of my own family office, I adopted this 30-day rule, and it revolutionized my approach. The rule instilled a sense of urgency, necessitating a continuous flow of potential deals to ensure I always had at least one lucrative investment opportunity ready.

Here's what happened: Before the 30-day rule, it took me ten years to achieve my first billion dollars in transaction value. After the 30-day rule, how long did it take me to reach my second billion? Just 18 months. And my third billion? Only 22 months. Granted, after hitting my fourth billion 12 months later, I did slow down a bit due to COVID and prevailing market conditions.

From 2018 to 2022, I averaged 2 to 3 transactions per month (buying & selling). The only effective way to handle such a substantial amount of money within a limited timeframe each month is by actively exploring investment opportunities. However, I must caution those new to real estate against hastily adopting the 30-day approach I employed.

Successfully deploying funds within a short period requires a crucial learning curve. It would be prudent for you to tailor your investment amounts and time frame to suit your specific circumstances. Creating a sense of urgency and establishing a well-defined time frame that aligns with your experience level is key. Seasoned investors may require a shorter reinvestment time, while those with less experience should consider allocating a longer period for reinvestment.

On a personal note, my wife, a successful musician, has no involvement in the real estate business. One day, she stumbled upon a YouTube video of an interview I did a couple of years ago when I hit my first billion. You'll find the video if you search "Curtis Haines Billionaire" on Google. During dinner, she asked me, "Are we billionaires?" I chuckled and replied, "Far from it. We have completed over a billion dollars in real estate transactions. We acquired those properties through partnerships with other families, meaning we have relatively small ownership stakes in each. However, that being said, we are multimillionaires."

Now, let's refocus on the family office concept. It's not about your current wealth; it's about transforming your mindset regarding money and investment decisions. I strongly encourage you to establish your own family office, regardless of your net worth. I've condensed the valuable lessons I learned from my mentor, Del Walmsley, and the family office concept into four crucial steps for building generational wealth:

1. Replace non-income-producing assets with income-producing assets.
2. Use leverage to acquire income-producing assets.
3. Capture equity gains early and reinvest.
4. Maximize your return on net worth and track annually.

The first step involves replacing non-income-producing assets with income-producing assets. A significant concept here is "income-producing assets." If you were to compare the asset lists of an average person (Joe) and a wealthy family, aside from the obvious size difference, you'd notice that Joe's assets consist mostly of non-income-producing assets, while the wealthy family's assets generate income. Chapter 5 will help you navigate through your family's assets and uncover additional investment capital.

Step two is to use leverage to acquire income-producing assets. Reflect on your upbringing and the beliefs you developed about debt. As we delve into the new strategy in Chapter 6, pay close attention to how the average Joe and wealthy families approach debt differently.

Step three emphasizes the importance of capturing equity gains early and reinvesting them. Del introduced me to the value-add cycle and shared best practices for enhancing a property's net operating income

(NOI) and value. We'll explore this concept further in Chapter 7, as it was one of the significant mistakes I made early in my real estate investment journey.

Step four focuses on maximizing the return on your net worth and tracking it annually. In Chapter 4, you will learn how to calculate your return on net worth, what form you should use, and how key financial statements will help you make needed course corrections. Step four will help you create your CEO scorecard.

Diversification

Many family offices typically maintain a diversified investment portfolio. The family office I came across was investing in different types of real estate, including multifamily, retail, office, and industrial. Most of their real estate was newer construction, and they also had some real estate development projects in their portfolio.

Apart from real estate, the family office appeared to have considerable investments in multiple small businesses operating in diverse industries. Although I didn't obtain the exact allocation percentages, I presumed they had a well-diversified portfolio. Similar to many affluent families, they did not accumulate their wealth through diversification.

If you were to speak with a financial advisor, they would suggest a particular approach to diversify your portfolio. This approach aims to decrease the likelihood of risk and safeguard against substantial losses. However, it may also restrict the potential for higher returns.

"Diversification is protection against ignorance. It makes little sense if you know what you are doing." –Warren Buffett

Diversification, while commonly advocated, is not always the best approach for investors who possess deep knowledge and understanding of the businesses they are investing in. Instead of spreading investments across a wide range of asset classes, Warren Buffett suggests focusing on a smaller number of carefully selected investments where you have a strong grasp of their underlying economic and competitive advantages.

My wealth was created from multifamily real estate investments. At one point in time, I had 99% of my assets in multifamily real estate. The more experience I gained, the more comfortable I became investing in one asset class.

Before investing your hard-earned money, putting in the effort required to build a solid foundation is essential. As CEO of your family office, you will be tasked with becoming an expert in one or two specific investment types. The best way to become comfortable with putting all of your eggs in one basket is to become a subject matter expert in that one basket. I cannot emphasize enough how crucial this point is. I have yet to encounter a person who achieved generational wealth through diversification alone.

Although these four steps to building generational wealth can be applied to any investment class or business, real estate offers one of the best paths to building wealth due to its tax advantages and accessibility to leverage for generating passive income.

Let's begin with step four because it ultimately serves as your overall guide to assessing your progress with the first three steps.

Chapter 4

Return on Net Worth

As we take a deep dive into your finances, keep in mind you are stepping into the shoes of a CEO in managing your family office without the support of a dedicated back-office team. The responsibility for this endeavor falls solely on you. It's more than just a shift in mindset; it's a bona fide business undertaking with the potential to significantly impact your family's wealth.

Personal Financial Statement

Just as with any successful enterprise, the ability to monitor and evaluate the overall health of your operation is crucial. Financial statements are vital to this assessment and play a key role in documenting a company's business activities and fiscal performance. In a similar vein, your personal financial statement will reflect the financial activities and performance of your family office.

To assist you in this process, I have provided a blank personal financial statement for your use, which can be downloaded from www.curtishaines.com.

Your personal financial statement will help you calculate your net worth and return on net worth. These two vital financial metrics are fundamental in assessing an individual's or a family's financial health and journey toward generational wealth.

Net worth is a fundamental measure of an individual's financial position. It is determined by calculating the difference between total assets and total liabilities. In simpler terms, it represents the value of all the assets owned after deducting all debts and obligations. Net worth is a powerful indicator of financial stability and is often considered a snapshot of your current financial standing.

Return on net worth is a critical financial ratio used to evaluate the profitability and efficiency of investments made with available capital. It measures the percentage of net income generated based on total net worth. Return on net worth reveals how effectively an individual or family utilizes their net worth to generate profits.

Pursuing generational wealth often requires a more informed approach than merely accumulating assets. Understanding the significance of both net worth and return on net worth empowers individuals and families to make strategic financial decisions, laying the foundation for long-term prosperity.

The average person often doesn't know their net worth or which form to use when asked. This lack of knowledge can be attributed, in part, to their differing approaches to the use of debt. Let me explain how the average Joe and wealthy families acquire debt. When the average Joe uses debt to purchase non-income-producing assets, they must present their W-2 form to qualify for a loan. Conversely, when you use debt to acquire income-producing assets like apartments, you'll need a personal financial statement (the form used to track your net worth).

If an entire industry was created around the personal financial statements of wealthy families, why is it not important enough to teach this basic concept in school? Despite having a background in accounting and being a certified public accountant with a master's in taxation, I had never encountered this concept until I entered the real estate industry. It's baffling to realize how little attention I paid to my assets before that. This revelation leaves me wondering why such a crucial concept was not part of my education until now. All right, let's refocus and get back on track.

Net Worth

So, what is your net worth? Begin by jotting down all of your assets. For now, don't worry about whether they are income-producing or non-income-producing assets. Include bank accounts, stocks, bonds,

CDs, your house, car, expensive jewelry, and any other real estate you possess. Next, list all your debts, such as credit card debt, student loans, mortgage, and car loans. Subtract your total debt from your total assets to determine your net worth. The personal financial statement is the recommended form for making this process easier to track.

Net Worth = Total Assets – Total Debt

Remember, the significance of your net worth lies not in its absolute size but in understanding your starting point and identifying the financial milestones required to attain true financial independence. Although earning six figures may seem like a measure of success, many people who earn that amount still struggle to make ends meet and live paycheck to paycheck. Merely achieving a specific net worth figure is not the ultimate measure of financial well-being either. What truly matters is how effectively you leverage your net worth and the extent to which it works for you.

Return on Net Worth

To accurately measure your financial progress, it's important to closely monitor and evaluate your return on net worth on an annual basis. By focusing on your return on net worth, you can gain valuable insights into how effectively your investments and financial decisions are contributing to generating passive income and improving your overall financial position. This shift in focus from simply accumulation to maximizing the potential of your net worth allows you to make informed and strategic choices toward achieving financial independence and generational wealth.

To determine your return on net worth, you can follow this simple calculation: Divide your passive income by your total net worth.

Return on Net Worth = Passive Income ÷ Net Worth

Passive income refers to money earned with minimal or no effort on a regular basis, distinct from active income, which is earned through active employment or self-employment. Active income is the compensation received for providing goods or services, typically in the form of wages, salaries, tips, commissions, bonuses, fees, pensions, and social security. Earned income is the result of direct effort and time spent working. These active income sources are not considered in the calculation.

On the other hand, passive income is typically generated from investments, rental properties, and business activities in which the individual is not materially participating. Passive income includes dividends, interest, real estate rentals, royalties, and certain types of businesses where the individual is not actively managing operations.

These passive income sources should be taken into account for the calculation.

For many individuals, the return on net worth will likely be less than 1%. Before I invested in real estate, my return on net worth was much lower than that and stood at just 0.161459%. While I did manage to accumulate some assets, they didn't generate significant income. My earnings were limited to a small amount from interest and dividends.

Once you start acquiring income-producing assets, you should see a nice year-over-year jump in your return on net worth within the first five years. In my case, my return on net worth increased to 1.6% in the first year. That might appear to be a small increase, but it represents a 900% year-over-year increase (1.6% divided by 0.161459%).

By the end of the fifth year, I achieved a peak return on net worth of 17%, far exceeding any of my earlier expectations. However, in the next four years, my return on net worth averaged 8.6% due to the mistakes I made in step three (capturing equity gains early and reinvesting). After making the necessary course corrections, my year-over-year return on net worth for the past six years trended higher at an average return on net worth of 16.97%. Despite the mistakes I made, my net worth has consistently increased year-over-year for the past 15 years.

If you do not see a year-over-year improvement in your return on net worth or an increase in your total net worth itself, something is off in one or more of the first three steps. Use this as a scorecard for you and your family to track yearly so you can easily make course corrections as needed.

Review the illustration below for a clear visualization of the essential concepts. The initial step is to establish your family office business. Like any business, a family office requires financial statements. Next, you will need to fill out your personal financial statement. Your personal financial statement serves as the core financial statement for your family office, providing a starting point and enabling you to monitor your net worth and return on net worth annually.

Lastly, you should document the annual changes in your net worth and return on net worth. By analyzing these year-over-year changes, you can determine how well you are maximizing the returns on your family's assets. These essential concepts will help you create a basic scorecard for your family office.

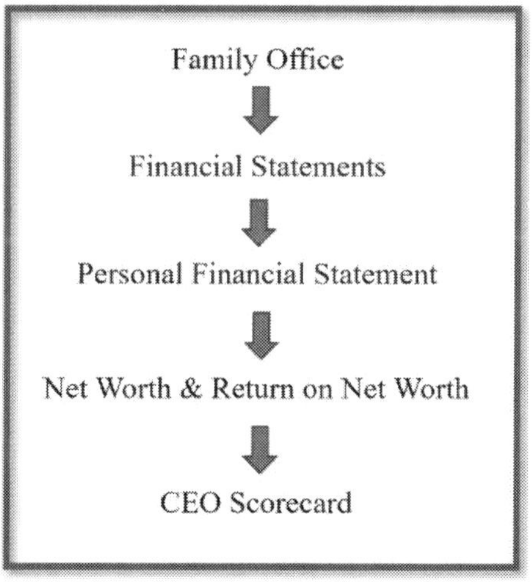

Financial Independence

We can also use return on net worth to help set realistic long-term goals toward achieving financial independence. Financial independence refers to a state in which an individual has attained a level of financial stability and security that allows them to cover their living expenses, lifestyle choices, and future goals without being reliant on active employment or external financial support. In other words, financially independent individuals have accumulated sufficient wealth, assets, and sources of income to sustain their desired way of life without the need for continuous employment or assistance from others.

Key aspects of financial independence include:

- Covering Expenses: A financially independent person can meet their daily living expenses, including housing, food, utilities, healthcare, transportation, and other necessities from their own financial resources.

- Lifestyle Choices: Financial independence provides the freedom to make choices based on personal preferences rather than on financial constraints. This could include pursuing hobbies, travel, leisure activities, and other lifestyle aspirations.

- Retirement: Financial independence often allows individuals to retire at a time of their choosing, as they have accumulated enough savings and investments to sustain themselves during their retirement years.

- Passive Income: Achieving financial independence often involves generating passive income from investments, real estate, business ventures, or other sources. Passive income flows in without requiring active participation in a traditional job.

- Emergency Preparedness: Financially independent individuals have a cushion to handle unexpected financial challenges, such as medical emergencies or economic downturns, without disrupting their overall financial stability.

- Generational Wealth: Achieving financial independence can also involve creating a legacy of wealth that can be passed on to future generations, providing them with opportunities and security.

It's important to note that the concept of financial independence can vary from person to person. Some may consider themselves financially independent when they have achieved a level of income that covers their basic needs, while others may have more ambitious goals, such as achieving a certain net worth or living a luxurious lifestyle without financial worries.

Ultimately, financial independence represents the ability to control one's financial destiny, make choices aligned with personal values and goals, and live life on one's own terms, free from the constraints of financial instability.

So, what do you need to achieve financial independence? Take a moment to calculate your number. Write down the amount necessary to cover your daily living expenses and desired lifestyle. Knowing your end goal will help guide you in your new role as CEO of your family office.

Suppose you need $45,000 a year to reach financial independence. You just completed your personal financial statement and calculated your net worth to be $500,000. In theory, all you need to do is invest that amount in an income-producing property that generates a 9% cash-on-cash return ($500,000 x 9% = $45,000). Sounds simple, right?

It can be challenging when the majority of your money is tied up in non-income-producing assets like your house and car. However, don't lose hope. Many of us began with few, if any, income-producing assets as well. At least you have identified a goal and know what you're working with.

Essentially, your assets aren't doing much to support you—you're the one putting in all the effort. Your objective is to reverse this dynamic and have your assets work harder on your behalf. The ultimate goal is to build cash flow. While many people consider wealth to be a large sum of money, financial independence is actually achieved through consistent cash flow rather than a mere accumulation of funds.

This strategy diverges greatly from conventional methods of retirement planning and investing, which we are all familiar with since early high school. The old formula is simple: begin investing as early as possible, ensure diversification of your portfolio, and save a substantial portion of your earned income, typically between 20 and 30%. It's funny how they left out the most important factor: die before your money runs out.

The old formula focuses on accumulating a specific amount of money before you retire. You need to save $1.5 million by age 65, for example. The new formula focuses on cash flow, not a pile of money.

In the next chapter, we will help you uncover additional investment capital, money used to invest in income-producing assets. As you progress through each step, you will realize the unique characteristics of real estate investing that will make it easier for you to reach your goals faster.

Chapter 5

Income-Producing Assets

As the CEO of your family office, your number one priority is to get your assets to work. You get your assets to work by replacing non-income-producing assets with income-producing ones. It is essential to embrace your new role as CEO and approach these decisions as business decisions. This business mindset will help you overcome any emotional attachments you might have towards non-income-producing assets. Let's thoroughly examine your personal financial statement to identify opportunities for additional investment capital.

Savings

While many individuals consider their savings account as a safety net for unexpected expenses, it's worth questioning whether you truly need such a substantial amount, like $25,000 or $50,000, for a rainy day. Consider delving into your savings account to obtain additional investment capital. This may be one of the more challenging decisions you'll face as the CEO of your family office.

Throughout your life, you've been taught the importance of saving money, and your savings account balance may represent a safety net, security blanket, or badge of honor passed down by your parents. However, it's important to note that wealthy families don't simply save their money; they invest it. A savings account is not an income-producing asset. Remember their mindset—they acquire assets that work for them. A savings account will barely cover bank fees, brokerage fees, and cost-of-living increases. Consider replacing your savings, IRAs, and 401(k)'s with income-producing assets.

Let's face it: The average person isn't doing an adequate job saving for retirement. The median retirement savings for working-age households in the US is approximately $95,776. This means half of households have more than this amount saved, while the other half have less. The average retirement savings, at $141,542, can be skewed by a few outliers who have saved a significant amount. Therefore, the median is a more accurate measure of most people's savings. According to a recent survey by Fidelity, Baby Boomers have an average of $112,000 saved, which is less than half of what they should have in the bank by age 60.

If you rely on Social Security to cover your retirement expenses, think again. The average Social Security check is around $1,800 monthly, less than $22,000 annually. On the other hand, the average 65-year-old American household spends over $4,000 per month or just over $48,000 per year. It's evident that the system is broken, and your expectations for your golden years may be far from reality.

"If you can't find a way to make money in your sleep, you will work until you die." –Warren Buffett

Expensive Toys

Expensive toys, gold, or jewelry are not income-producing assets. I know someone whose neighbor owns a lavish RV that sits in their driveway year after year, collecting dust. It's likely that they also have a significant loan on that RV. Not only does this asset fail to generate any income, but it also costs the family thousands of dollars in cash flow each year. Now is the time to downsize your lifestyle and focus on building real wealth. Stop living beyond your means and refrain from using leverage to purchase things you can't afford.

There will be plenty of time to enjoy luxuries once you achieve your financial goals and build real wealth. We lived well below our means during the first five years in real estate. I used to say that we were cash poor because every penny we earned was promptly reinvested back into real estate.

Jim Rohn once asked, "Do you know the difference between the rich and the poor?" The poor spend their money first and save what's left, while the rich invest their money first and spend what's left. Although this quote originated in the 1980s, it remains relevant today. I would modify it slightly with easy access to consumer debt, stating that the poor spend their money first, and anything left over goes to paying down credit card debt.

Equity from Other Real Estate

I was taught that paying off your debt was a good thing. During one of my first training sessions at Lifestyles, I remember Del asking the attendees to raise their hands if they had paid off their home mortgage. I proudly raised my hand, feeling accomplished and excited to share my achievement. However, Del immediately pointed at me and said, "You are an idiot." I looked around the room, puzzled, wondering if I had misunderstood the question. What did I do wrong? Now I understand. Now I get it.

All of us were taught to pay off our debt, but this mindset can make it difficult for some of you to make another challenging decision—taking out a new mortgage on your home. If you have only partially paid down your mortgage, you might need to refinance into a larger loan.

A HELOC (home equity line of credit) might be a more palatable option for those still struggling with adding a new mortgage to their home. When you close on your HELOC, you don't have a mortgage balance or any mortgage payments. A HELOC is a line of credit attached to your checking account. You can access funds from this line of credit as needed and choose when and how much to borrow. You will only pay interest on the amount you have withdrawn.

My house doubled in value between the time I bought it in 2004 and joined Lifestyles in 2008, allowing me to leverage my original equity through a HELOC. Keep in mind a HELOC is a variable rate loan. You want to avoid variable-rate loans in a rising-rate environment.

Selling Other Real Estate

In some cases, selling your real estate might be necessary to capture additional investment capital. I know a family that has been holding onto land for two generations. Each generation had plans to build a home on their family's land but never did. The land is located in a lovely picturesque area but just a little too far away from basic necessities. Building substantial wealth for yourself, your family, and future generations is far more important.

If you've been holding onto land for years, intending to build your dream home, it's time to sell it. Not only does it fail to generate income, but it also drains your cash flow through property taxes. Do you own a second vacation home or a small lake house that you only use once a year? Sell it. You should consider tapping into your home's equity or any other real estate to access additional investment capital.

Making these decisions takes work. However, you don't have to make all the decisions today. If you already have sufficient cash in your account to get started, you don't have to convert everything to cash immediately. Nor do you have to make all the decisions about your retirement accounts right away. Begin with what you have now, and as you see the results from your initial investment, making more challenging decisions will become easier.

Remember, as CEO of your family office, you need to become an expert in one or two specific investment types. Real estate offers one of the best paths to building wealth due to its tax advantages and accessibility to leverage for generating passive income. I recommend obtaining a thorough understanding and expertise in either single-family, multifamily, or both.

As I look back on my journey, I am astonished by the number of limiting beliefs I held. I used to believe that I needed a job to make money, that hard work and saving were the only paths to financial stability, that living debt-free was the best way, that the stock market was the key to building wealth, that diversifying my investments was necessary, and that saving for retirement was the only way to secure my future. I also thought that having a million dollars meant I was rich, and that I needed a sledgehammer for real estate investments. I never even considered owning apartments—you don't know what you don't know.

Stop trading time for money. Get your assets to work so you don't have to. One of the most challenging things to do is to recognize our limiting beliefs. As Henry Ford said, "If you always do what you've always done, you'll always get what you've always got." I shared a few of my limiting beliefs. Which ones are holding you back?

Let me emphasize one final point before we move on to the next chapter. Many of us struggle with a specific four-letter word today, especially considering the extensive media coverage it receives. Care to guess what that word is? It's "rich." Some people find it difficult to reconcile with the idea of becoming wealthy, as they associate it with negative connotations, like greed and ruthlessness. However, it's important to remember that not all rich individuals embody these traits, just as not all poor individuals are virtuous. The amount of money one possesses is not the sole determinant of one's character. It's about personal growth and how one utilizes their wealth.

Financial independence is about gaining the freedom to pursue what you truly desire. It could mean spending more quality time with family, going on vacations, or giving back to others. Helping others lies at the core of what makes Lifestyles Unlimited so successful. Del's system builds wealth in the service of others, not at the expense of others. So, for those of you who may be hesitant due to negative associations with that four-letter word, I encourage you to reconsider and challenge all of your belief systems.

Chapter 6

Use Leverage to Acquire Income-Producing-Assets

Leverage can be a powerful tool for building wealth or destroying wealth. In this chapter, we will delve into the distinction between good loans and bad loans and explore how our perception of debt and asset accumulation differs from that of high-net-worth families.

Bad Leverage

You may be familiar with credit cards, which can charge exorbitant interest rates up to 36%. But you might not be well-acquainted with title loans or payday loans, as these are typically accessed by individuals in dire financial circumstances. If you find yourself in need of a quick loan, you can visit any of the conveniently located title loan stores. They offer loans based on the value of your car, using your car's title as collateral. The interest rates for such loans range from 169% to a staggering 300%.

And if that wasn't bad enough, there are hundreds of thousands of conveniently located payday loan stores where you can obtain a loan based on your monthly paycheck stub, but the interest rates on these loans can reach up to 1,500%. It becomes evident that individuals burdened by these bad loans are often just one unexpected expense away from missing their rent or car payment.

How Wealthy Families Use Leverage

From an early age, we are taught that going to school, securing a job, buying a nice house and car, and eventually retiring are the key milestones of a successful life. Moreover, we are also taught that all loans are bad and should be paid off as soon as possible. While it is true that certain loans, such as those with high interest rates like credit cards, should be prioritized for repayment, this perception that all loans are inherently bad can lead to some suboptimal financial decisions. Some individuals even go to the extreme of paying off their home mortgages or, worse, buying income-producing assets entirely with cash, believing that being debt-free is a mark of financial success.

So, what is the point? Most of us use leverage to acquire assets beyond our means, while wealthy families use leverage to acquire income-producing assets. While the average person works hard to accumulate assets, wealthy families acquire assets that work hard for them. Do you see the disparity in how different groups perceive and utilize assets? Can you grasp how leverage is employed differently by high-net-worth families?

The average individual's primary income source stems from their J-O-B. The more money they earn, the more expensive things they tend to acquire in an attempt to keep up with the proverbial "Joneses." A bigger house, a nicer car—these are the markers of their success. However, relying solely on their job income to afford such luxuries often leads them to accumulate debt to acquire assets beyond their means. By the time they retire, they often find themselves without sufficient funds to sustain their lifestyle.

In contrast, income-producing assets are the primary source of funds for wealthy families. The income generated by these assets is paying down loans and providing cash flow. Wealthy families build generational wealth that grows over time and supports their family for future generations.

Leverage in Real Estate

It is apparent that the lower an individual's income, the higher the interest rates they will have to bear. Title loans and payday loans are extreme examples, charging exorbitant interest rates due to the increased risk associated with defaults. As one ascends the financial ladder, the relationship between income and interest rates becomes less noticeable.

It is safe to assume that someone like Warren Buffett would secure a car loan at a lower interest rate than you or me. Similarly, most wealthy families enjoy a competitive advantage even when it comes to business loans. Small business owners understand the challenges of obtaining a loan, with their ability to secure financing relying solely on their creditworthiness. It is difficult to compete against a wealthy business owner when you are paying a 9% interest rate while they are paying a mere 3%.

The good news is that we are on a level playing field with wealthy families in obtaining loans for multifamily properties. The real estate industry offers an encouraging aspect in terms of interest rates. As real estate investors, we can secure the same lower interest rates that wealthy families enjoy because the properties we invest in are income-producing assets. Real estate loans are more accessible, even for first-time owners, as lenders place greater emphasis on the projected income of the property rather than solely focusing on the borrower's financial profile.

Competitive Advantage

Additionally, we have a competitive advantage over wealthy families due to our hands-on approach to managing our properties. Our ability to make significant improvements in day-to-day operations and implement strategic tweaks increases our investments' value and equity gains. In contrast, wealthy families often rely on large national third-party management companies, which may have a different level of attention to detail.

For example, my first acquisition was purchased from the second-largest real estate investment trust (REIT) in the country. Their utility expense was averaging $23,000 a month. After we took over the property, we renegotiated a better electricity rate and implemented a water conservation program. Our average utility expense was reduced to $13,800 a month, increasing our net operating income (NOI) by $110,400 and our value by $1.84 million.

$$\$110{,}400 \text{ NOI} \uparrow \div 6\% \text{ Cap Rate} = \$1.84 \text{ million Value} \uparrow$$

Net operating income is the difference between the property's income and expenses. If you increase income or lower expenses, you will increase NOI. An increase in NOI will increase value.

Every business has a way to calculate value. For multifamily real estate, NOI divided by cap rate determines value. Cap rate is the return you expect to make if you buy with all cash. I will cover cap rates in a little more detail later in the book.

$$\text{Cap Rate} = \text{NOI} \div \text{Value}$$

Our hands-on approach to managing our properties enables us to extract more value than larger national operators. We can also level the playing field with the larger amount of capital needed to buy bigger properties. By pooling resources with other like-minded investors, we can collectively acquire larger assets, providing us with greater economies of scale. The stronger our economies of scale, the easier it becomes to enhance our net operating income and capture additional equity gains.

Leverage in multifamily loans offers distinct advantages over single-family loans, and one of the notable aspects is its independence from the need for a W-2 job as a qualifying factor. This distinction stems from the fundamental difference in how multifamily loans are underwritten compared to single-family loans.

In single-family loans, a W-2 job is often a critical component of the underwriting process. Lenders typically assess an individual borrower's creditworthiness, debt-to-income ratio, and ability to repay the loan based on their employment status and income history. A traditional single-family mortgage lender may require proof of stable employment, a consistent income stream, and a strong credit score to approve a loan. This approach is grounded in the belief that an individual borrower's financial stability and income are essential for loan repayment.

On the other hand, multifamily loans are underwritten with a unique perspective. These loans are primarily evaluated based on the property's financial performance and ability to generate sufficient income to cover the loan payments. The lender assesses factors such as the property's rental income, operating expenses, vacancy rates, and potential for future rental growth. This approach shifts the emphasis away from an individual borrower's employment status or W-2 income and places it on the income-generating potential of the multifamily property.

In addition, there are more multifamily lenders who underwrite loans above $10 million than those below $1 million. As you gain more multifamily experience, acquiring more properties becomes easier. I carry over $1.4 billion in debt on my balance sheet. I am the guarantor for most of these loans, which means I am personally responsible if any of them default. Remember, before real estate, I was the guy who paid off my house mortgage because that was what I was taught at an early age.

So, why am I not concerned about having this much debt now? It's because all of these loans are self-collateralized by income-producing assets. The properties generate sufficient income to pay down the loans, and their value far exceeds the loan balances. In other words, they are low-leverage investments with an average loan-to-value ratio below 64%. Moreover, all of these loans are structured under the Operating Entity

LLC, meaning they do not appear on my personal credit report and do not impact my credit score.

The Benefits of Leverage

Let's explore a couple of examples that highlight the significance of leverage. For instance, suppose you purchased an apartment complex for $4 million with all cash and later sold it for $5 million, resulting in a $1 million profit.

$5,000,000	Proceeds from sale
-$4,000,000	Original cash down
$1,000,000	Profit

Now, let's imagine you bought the same apartment complex using leverage, with a $1 million cash down payment and a $3 million loan. If you sell for $5 million, your profit would still be $1 million.

$5,000,000	Proceeds from sale
-$3,000,000	Loan
-$1,000,000	Original cash down
$1,000,000	Profit

At first glance, both examples might seem to yield the same result: a $1 million profit. However, as the CEO of your family office, your primary focus is to ensure your assets work for you. The harder your assets work, the faster you can accumulate generational wealth. Let's compare the return on investment (ROI) in both examples.

Using all cash, the $4 million down payment generated a 25% ROI ($1 million profit divided by $4 million cash down payment). In contrast, when leveraging was employed, the $1 million cash down payment resulted in a 100% ROI ($1 million profit divided by $1 million cash down payment). In other words, in the second example, your $1 million cash asset worked four times harder than your $4 million cash asset.

Instead of using $4 million in all cash to buy one property, consider buying four properties using leverage, each potentially generating $1 million in profit. This demonstrates the concept of working four times harder through leverage.

Don't let the extra zeros distract you from grasping this crucial distinction. The outcomes remain the same even if you eliminate a few zeros. Instead of considering a $4,000,000 apartment, imagine a $400,000 single-family rental. With a $100,000 cash down payment, your money will work four times as hard compared to paying all cash. To further emphasize the point, let's remove a few more zeros. You can collectively purchase the apartment by pooling your $10,000 with other like-minded families. Your $10,000 investment in the partnership will work four times as hard using leverage compared to buying all cash.

Leverage can be a powerful tool when used strategically. We can make better financial decisions by understanding the difference between good and bad loans and recognizing how high-net-worth families view assets and utilize leverage differently.

While the average person relies on their job income and accumulates debt to acquire assets, high-net-worth families use leverage to obtain income-producing assets that contribute to building generational wealth.

"Get your ass to work or get your assets to work."
–Curtis Haines

Chapter 7

Capture Equity Gains Early and Redeploy

The previous chapter discussed the importance of using leverage to buy income-producing properties. The leverage is what helps create exponential gains from your investment. When we add value to the property, we don't have to double the value to double our returns. With leverage, we only have to add incremental value to gain exponential returns.

Value Add with Leverage

My mentor, Del Walmsley, has taught me the art of adding value to my properties. Through his guidance, I have come to understand the significance of the value-add cycle and the velocity of money. I have gained expertise in property acquisition, property improvement, and property management. One of the essential elements Del emphasized for achieving success is providing the best product at the best price and with the best service. To establish a strong foundation in the art of value add, an educational and mentoring group like Lifestyles Unlimited is indispensable. This chapter will focus on the importance of value adds, not the details behind how to create value add.

As you accumulate income-producing assets, monitoring your return on equity versus your cash-on-cash returns becomes essential to determine how hard your assets are working for you. Let me illustrate the big mistake I made during my early real estate investments by providing two examples that closely resembled one of my acquisitions.

Suppose you purchased an apartment complex for $4 million with a $1 million cash down payment and a $3 million loan. Let's assume the property generates $150,000 in annual cash flow. In this case, the property would yield a 15% cash-on-cash return ($150,000 cash flow divided by $1 million equity).

$4,000,000 FMV
-$3,000,000 Debt
$1,000,000 Equity

$150,000 Cash Flow
15% Cash on Cash Return ($150,000 cash flow / $1 million equity)

Now, let's fast forward to the end of the third year. Suppose you have increased the property's net operating income, and its value has risen to $7 million. Although you might hesitate to sell because of the strong 15% cash-on-cash returns, it's crucial to consider the return on equity. After increasing the property's value to $7 million, the return on equity would be only 3.75% ($150,000 cash flow divided by $4 million equity).

$7,000,000 New FMV
-$3,000,000 Debt
$4,000,000 Equity

$150,000 Cash Flow
3.75% Return on Equity ($150,000 cash flow / $4 million equity)

Realizing that you can find other properties that can generate returns greater than 3.75% highlights the importance of monitoring your return on equity. Doing so lets you optimize your investment decisions and maximize your wealth.

My Biggest Mistake

Reflecting on my journey, the concept of family offices profoundly impacted me, particularly step three, capturing equity gains early and redeploying them. I received numerous calls each month from brokers inquiring if I had any interest in selling my property. Our average cash-on-cash returns consistently exceeded 15%. While it was possible to find other properties with similar returns, the current one we owned required minimal effort on our part to continue generating nice cash-on-cash returns.

We had already put in the hard work repositioning the property. We fixed everything upfront, ensuring that there were no major repairs looming that would impact our cash flow. Moreover, we had secured an attractive loan for the property, and it was situated in a robust rental market. We enjoyed favorable economies of scale with or without this property. Consequently, I found no compelling reason to sell and quickly disregarded the broker inquiries. My focus was on purchasing properties rather than selling them.

I had already made difficult decisions regarding my non-income-producing assets and had successfully used leverage and acquired more income-producing assets. However, I made the mistake of not properly tracking my return on equity. While I enjoyed high cash-on-cash returns, my return on equity remained in the low single digits. Yes, my assets were out there working for me, but in reality, they were not working very hard over time.

Over the following years, I decided to sell my entire Galleria portfolio. It wasn't an easy choice, as I had developed an emotional attachment to this portfolio. It has served as the catalyst for my professional growth and achieving success. Accumulating such a significant number of assets in a robust rental market was no small feat. Ultimately, it was the right business decision to proceed with the sales. Without being introduced to the family office concept, my return on net worth would likely have remained stagnant for a few more years before declining. Although not a bad position to be in, the family office concept aims to leave a lasting legacy for future generations.

Build Momentum

As the CEO of your family office, it is crucial to monitor all your income-producing assets, identify opportunities to add value quickly, and capture those gains through cash-out refinancing or sales. Leverage good debt and reinvest the tax-free distributions into more income-producing assets, continuing the value-add cycle. The ability to swiftly repeat this value-add cycle will create increasing momentum in building true wealth.

"You can't get rich slow." –Del Walmsley

Consider the initial five years of your real estate journey as the foundation for building wealth. The greater momentum you can generate during this period, the quicker you will achieve financial independence. The extent to which you wish to capitalize on that momentum is entirely your choice. Eventually, when you deem it appropriate, you can gradually ease off the value-add cycle and instead focus on holding your properties for longer durations.

I was able to quickly recover from my mistakes by selling the properties with the most unrealized equity gains, particularly those that had already undergone a strong value-add strategy. Recovering from an early mistake can be challenging if your investment objectives do not align with the property's investment goals. This is where your expertise in a specific investment class can significantly impact your success.

If you didn't understand the difference between a yield play and a value play, for example, and assumed all real estate transactions were value plays, your initial investment might get stuck in a long-term hold. Hard to gain momentum during your first five years when you are holding one property for 7–10 years. It is crucial to consider each property's unique characteristics and ask yourself if its investment returns align with your personal investment goals.

From my experience, I have learned that location plays an important role in the success of a property. Yes, a portfolio of properties helped improve our economies of scale, but the real key to our success was the location of the portfolio. Properties in good locations are more likely to weather economic downturns, and when the market recovers, those in strong rental submarkets tend to see the greatest upside.

As I ventured into other cities and partnered with other owner-operators, I expanded my standards to include three factors: quality asset, quality location, and quality operator. If a property satisfies these criteria and its investment returns match my personal investment objectives, I feel assured in my investment choice. Let's spend a little more time on these three criteria in the next chapter.

Chapter 8

My Three Qs

I grew up in a military family, and we lived in various places around the world. We spent a few years in Turkey and England before settling in San Antonio, Texas. Unfortunately, I was too young to remember any of those experiences. We traveled a lot during my childhood, which probably explains why I'm not a big fan of traveling now. Eventually, I moved to Houston, Texas, and I don't plan on leaving anytime soon.

I'm very familiar with Houston and know all about the local economy, submarkets, neighborhoods, and schools. I've driven by or analyzed practically every apartment complex built in the 70s and 80s.

When a property goes up for sale, I can easily estimate its worth based on my past experience.

Buying properties close to home has become second nature to me. However, as I've expanded my portfolio to other cities, I've come to realize how challenging it can be to invest in unfamiliar locations. How can you make a wise investment decision when you know nothing about the area? To help me navigate the world beyond Texas, I've come up with my Three Qs—quality asset, quality location, quality operator.

Repositioning Strategies

We have to look at quality asset and quality location at the same time because location will determine how much room we may or may not have to turn a property into a quality asset. To better understand what makes a property a quality asset, let us delve deeper into rehab and possible repositioning strategies.

To increase the value and improve the positioning of our properties, we utilize capital improvements and address operational inefficiencies. Sometimes, the biggest impact we can have is simply to run the property better and provide better service.

Our approach involves both improving operations and upgrading the property. Our rehab budget categorizes issues into life safety, deferred maintenance, and upgrades. Life safety issues such as trip hazards, loose railings, and exposed electrical wiring are prioritized as they could potentially harm someone.

Deferred maintenance issues are all the wear and tear of a property that is not considered life safety issues. Deferred maintenance issues left untouched for years could easily become life safety issues. Replacing all wood rot throughout the property, replacing the roofs, replacing old air conditioners (A/C), and replacing old boilers would fall in the deferred maintenance category.

Upgrades are the key to most repositioning strategies and will directly impact our ability to raise rents. Upgrades can enhance curb appeal and help make the best first impressions. Adding an amenity, painting the exterior, or upgrading the leasing office and interior units would fall under the upgrades category.

Most issues with a property can be fixed. Our only limitation is cost. We don't want to overpay on a property. Overpaying would include your total all-in cost—the purchase price plus rehab. It is important to fix any life safety issues and deferred maintenance issues. This is one of Del's golden rules—fix everything up front. If the cost becomes too high after fixing everything upfront, we will not proceed with the deal.

A light repositioning strategy could simply be fixing everything upfront and improving operations. However, upgrading the units with granite countertops, for example, may not be effective in increasing rent because of the property's location.

Remember, it's important to consider both the quality of the asset and its location simultaneously, as the location can impact the potential for turning a property into a quality asset. To begin, let's establish what constitutes a quality asset.

Quality Asset

Determining what is a quality asset can be a complex task. While a new Class A property may seem obvious, it's often not that straightforward. To help navigate this process, I've identified some key factors I consider when evaluating assets. Certain issues with a property may be impossible to remedy, while others may simply be too costly to address. These are all important factors to remember when assessing an asset's quality. In general, I avoid properties that have window A/C units, a chiller A/C system, too many micro-units, or all one-bedroom units.

Most properties with window units would be categorized as "Class D" or, as most brokers would call it, a "very tired C." These properties usually have lower market rents, and there's a ceiling on how much you can charge. Increasing the rent beyond this point is challenging without significantly changing the property. If the submarket allows it, replacing the window units with split A/C systems or central

A/C is the best course of action. In other words, the property would have to be in a quality location to support this upgrade.

Think of a chiller system as one giant air-conditioning unit that services the entire property. Hospitals, schools, and large commercial buildings have chiller A/C systems. The main difference is they use four pipes to cool and heat. Most apartments only have two pipes to cool and heat. With a two-pipe system, you can only have either cool or hot air running, and it can take up to eight hours to switch from one to the other. This delay can be a problem in areas like Texas, where frequent and sudden weather changes leave residents unhappy during certain times of the year.

The high cost of maintenance and repairs is another issue with chiller A/C systems, which were phased out of use in apartments in the late 1960s. As a result, most of these buildings' piping systems and mechanical components are over 60 years old, making them prone to leaks and other failures. The best solution for a property with a chiller system is to replace it with central A/C, provided the submarket can support it.

A property having too many micro-units can be problematic. Apartment units with less than 450 sq. ft. in size are considered micro-units. Generally, residents living in micro-units are price sensitive, which puts a cap on rental rates. In some locations, upgrading the interior can allow for slightly higher rental rates. However, once a certain price point is reached, residents may choose to move to larger units elsewhere. Micro-units are usually difficult to fix, as the only way to do so is by combining two units into one by removing a wall. This is often not financially viable unless the property is purchased at a price significantly below market value.

Properties primarily consisting of one-bedroom units tend to attract residents looking for a temporary living situation. This type of resident base has a higher turnover rate than other submarkets, meaning that property owners must spend more money preparing units for new residents. Such residents view their apartments as a short-term solution and are typically price-sensitive, similar to those who prefer micro-units. If the rent prices are too high, they will quickly move to another property to find a more affordable option. It's important to note that having an unfavorable mix of unit types cannot be easily remedied.

Remember, the location will play a significant part in determining a quality asset. If the property is in a high-quality location, I might be good with micro-units or too many one-bedrooms. I know of an owner-operator who has an apartment with units less than 450 square feet. They are always 100% full because of location. And I will buy a property with a chiller system in a high-quality location because I can easily justify the cost of removing the chiller and converting the property to central A/C.

I almost forgot to mention parking. Limited parking is another property issue that is nearly impossible to remedy. Limited parking is typically found in older properties located in highly desirable locations.

In Houston, the minimum required number of parking spaces for apartments can range from 1.33 spaces for each one-bedroom unit to 2.0 spaces for each apartment unit with three or more bedrooms. Older properties are grandfathered in and typically have less than 1.25 parking spaces per apartment unit, regardless of the number of bedrooms.

A property with limited parking would not be considered a quality asset. For example, I quickly walked away from a 70-unit apartment with 70 two-bedroom units and 70 parking spaces. Under the current code, the property should have around 116 parking spaces. In other words, the property had 40% fewer parking spaces needed to maintain normal operations. The property was in a great location but struggled to maintain occupancy because of the limited parking on the property and no alternative parking outside the property.

Quality Location

For me, location is the most crucial factor when investing in real estate. The better the location, the more protected I am from significant market fluctuations. This is why I believe timing the market is unnecessary when investing in quality locations. Properties in prime areas tend to perform well in bullish and bearish markets. Additionally, assets in quality locations have a higher potential for appreciation than those in other locations.

I learned this firsthand when I purchased my first property shortly after the market collapsed in late 2008. Although initially apprehensive, this experience taught me to continue investing even after the oil collapse in late 2014. Thus, I am confident that I will continue investing in quality locations, regardless of current market conditions, because asset values will appreciate over time. However, it is important to note that even in a prime location, purchasing at the right price and with the right leverage is crucial. A bad deal can never be compensated by a good location.

So, what makes a quality location? When considering a location, examining it on multiple levels is important. First, at the city level, ask yourself about the local economic drivers and how a national correction might impact them. Research the city's major companies and industries with the most employees to gain insight into the local economy.

Be cautious of tertiary locations that rely heavily on only one company or industry, as this could pose a potential risk in an economic downturn. In general, larger cities tend to be more diverse and have stronger economic drivers, making them preferable. Next, examine the submarket level, followed by the neighborhood and street level, to ensure the location meets your specific needs.

When analyzing submarkets, it is important to determine which ones are strong and which ones are weak. A submarket can be thought of as a group of neighborhoods within a city. To identify the strongest submarkets, consider areas with positive trends and new development, such as new homes, retail stores, commercial properties, and infrastructure. These developments often lead to new job opportunities and further positive trends within the submarket, resulting in increasing occupancy and rent rates. On the other hand, weak submarkets may have vacant gas stations, retail centers, or businesses, indicating a lack of growth. In larger cities, identifying submarkets may require more extensive research than in smaller cities.

It's important to avoid high-crime areas, such as those with gang or drug activity, as well as areas with graffiti and other signs of criminal activity. While it's usually easy to spot high-crime areas when driving around the neighborhood, some larger cities may have an entire submarket that's considered high crime. As a rule of thumb, it's best to avoid these areas altogether.

When driving to the property, take note of how easy or difficult it was to find the property. Is it on a dead-end or side street with limited traffic, or a busy street with great frontage? Is the leasing office visible from the street? If you're on the fence about the neighborhood, it may be easier to pass on a property that's located on a dead-end street. If the property is located in a desirable submarket and neighborhood, it could still be a viable option, even if it's situated on a dead-end street.

It's also important to consider the general feel of the neighborhood. Does it have an industrial or residential feel, and who are the neighbors? Are any questionable businesses or eyesores nearby, such as empty buildings or overgrown vacant lots? Keep in mind that the neighborhood cannot be changed, and even large institutional investors have failed in attempts to improve neighborhoods with taxpayer funds.

The surrounding schools and school districts can also significantly impact the property's value over time. It's important to know the boundaries of the surrounding schools and whether the property is near any good schools. Convenience is also key, so consider what's within walking distance, such as schools, churches, grocery stores, restaurants, shopping, bus stops, parks, and other local businesses. Properties located near schools tend to have better occupancy rates, even if the school district is considered average.

Overall, location is the most important variable to consider when investing in real estate. It's best to invest in familiar locations where you feel comfortable and understand the area well.

Quality Operator

Defining what makes a quality operator can be tricky, much like finding the perfect employee. As someone who has worked in the staffing industry for 14 years, I've seen countless tests given to job seekers, ranging from IQ tests to personality assessments. Companies have spent large sums of money to develop the right interview questions and processes to select the best employees. However, based on my years of experience working with both Fortune 500 companies and small businesses, it's essentially a coin toss whether or not an employee will succeed. To improve your chances of selecting a quality operator, I can offer some general guidelines that may be helpful.

As a general rule, I am cautious about investing with owner-operators who live in one city/state but buy a property in another city/state. However, there are some exceptions to this rule. If the property is located within a two-hour radius, or if the owner-operator already owns a property nearby and has been self-managing for several years, I may consider investing with them. That being said, I still have reservations about investing with out-of-town owners. I would prefer to invest with experienced owner-operators who live in the same city as the property they buy.

It's important to remember that previous success does not necessarily guarantee future success. However, I am more confident in an owner-operator's abilities if they have a good track record, especially if they have completed at least one successful multifamily transaction. A history of multiple successful transactions is even more reassuring. That being said, I would still consider investing with a first-time owner-operator if they demonstrate strong business skills.

I'm interested to know the amount of cash they intend to invest. It's important for me to see a significant equity investment in proportion to their total net worth. I don't want to invest more than they are willing to contribute.

What is their business strategy? Specifically, do they focus on acquiring properties nationwide or in a particular location? Are they in a fast-paced acquisition mode? Do they specialize in deep value plays with shorter holding periods or in value plays with longer holding periods? If their properties are spread out, managing them effectively could be a challenge, and their resources may be stretched thin. However, if they concentrate on specific areas, they could benefit from economies of scale and manage their properties more efficiently.

Additionally, it's important to consider how often they acquire new properties. Ideally, no more than two transactions per year would be preferred. If they are acquiring properties too quickly, it could indicate that they are more interested in the next deal rather than managing their current investments properly. Lastly, it is crucial to note that value plays and yield plays require very different skill sets. Knowing the distinction between these two factors alone can significantly affect your investment outcomes. Understanding all of these differences is at the heart of a good mentor and training program.

Earlier, I mentioned that it was a coin flip whether the employee would make a good hire or not. However, conducting reference checks consistently improved our chances of finding the right fit. I like to call this "word on the street." What is the word on the street about the owner-operator? It's important to gather information about the owner-operator from multiple sources. The more people you can talk to, the higher the likelihood of selecting a quality operator.

Real Estate Syndications

When you start investing with another owner-operator, you are venturing into the realm of syndications. Real estate syndication is a business strategy used in the real estate industry, where multiple investors combine their finances and expertise to invest in and manage large real estate projects that would be difficult to undertake alone. This approach provides investors with access to opportunities that may be too large, complex, or costly for an individual to pursue.

In a real estate syndication, there are two main roles: the syndicator or general partner (GP), who originates the investment opportunity, conducts due diligence, secures financing, manages the project, and creates the investment structure and offerings for potential investors, and the limited partner (LP), who contributes capital to the syndication and receives returns on their investment based on the terms established in the syndication agreement.

Real estate syndications can take various forms, such as partnerships, limited liability companies, limited partnerships, or real estate investment trusts (REITs). The structure chosen can affect investor involvement, liability, tax implications, and potential for liquidity. Benefits of real estate syndication include access to larger and potentially more profitable real estate projects, diversification of real estate portfolios, shared expertise, passive investment, and economies of scale.

Investors interested in real estate syndication should evaluate the GP's track record, investment strategy, deal terms, and potential risks before investing. Due diligence and a clear understanding of the syndication structure are crucial for making informed investment decisions.

Based on my experience, I suggest investing in real estate as a general partner (GP) or as an independent rental owner. A small partnership where you have full control is also a good option. This will help you achieve financial independence more quickly. If you choose to invest as a limited partner (LP), be prepared to conduct extra research and due diligence. I recommend only investing in syndications as an LP within Lifestyles Unlimited, as Del Walmsley has created rules that protect LPs from some of the risks associated with outside syndications.

Most deals outside of Lifestyles use the limited partnership structure, where the syndicator (GP) has complete control, and the passive investors (LPs) have no voting rights. In contrast, deals inside Lifestyles are required to use the limited liability company structure, which gives passive investors important voting rights, including the ability to remove the syndicator. This kind of voting power is rare in outside deals.

Outside deals often use complex structures, such as distribution waterfalls, preferred equity, targeted bonuses, minimum GP draws, and various fees, including up-front fees, disposition fees, construction fees, and consulting fees. These types of structures limit the upside for passive investors and are prohibited inside of Lifestyles.

Cap Rates

One of the more difficult concepts to understand in real estate is cap rates. Net operating income (NOI) divided by cap rate determines a property's value. Remember, cap rate is the return you expect to make if you buy with all cash. The higher the cap rate, the higher the risk; conversely, the lower the cap rate, the lower the risk. Generally, prime locations and high-quality assets will have lower cap rates and higher property values, while poor locations and older assets will have higher cap rates and lower property values. However, cap rates are market-driven and vary widely based on location and current market conditions.

I am suspect of any cap rate used to support current or future property values. Instead, I recommend using your own cap rate based on your experience and the location of the property. A mortgage broker can provide you with a good starting cap rate for the area. You can adjust their cap rate based on your experience and location. Investing in locations you know well can be a great starting point. As you learn more about how to evaluate a property, you can branch out into other locations.

In the next chapter, you will learn about the tax benefits of real estate, which will further reinforce the advantages of investing in this asset class. Remember, leverage is what helps create exponential gains from your investment. Implementing the right tax strategy helps create exponential growth from your tax-deferred distributions

Chapter 9

Tax Advantages of Real Estate

Before we delve into the topic of taxes, take a moment to refresh yourself with a cup of coffee and return to this section of the book fully awake and ready to take notes. What I'm about to reveal is not commonly taught in college classes or shared by friends and family. I will show you the magic secret of how the wealthy amass more wealth through real estate investing. If I were a magician, I would be accused of showing you a behind-the-scenes look at how that magic trick works. I will share a part of my personal tax return to drive home this point.

Tax-Deferred Income

When Del began explaining the tax advantages of real estate, I became incredibly excited. As a good friend of mine would say, "pee in my pants excited." You see, before getting involved in real estate, I owned a small business, and at its peak, we were paying over $700,000 in taxes to the IRS each year. Imagine what a small business owner could achieve with an additional $700,000 annually. I never thought I could run a much larger business and not pay ANY taxes.

In the real estate business realm, a significant portion of the income from apartments can be shielded from federal income tax. When done correctly, most distributions you receive from your multifamily real estate investment will be tax-free. Technically, these distributions are tax-deferred because when you eventually sell the asset, you may be required to pay taxes. Nevertheless, you can also employ strategies to avoid paying taxes on the sale. Also, remember that partner distributions from cash-out refinances are always tax-free.

K-1 Income vs. Partner Distributions

It's important to understand the distinction between K-1 income and partner distributions. Therefore, I will take a few minutes to discuss taxes and how income and distributions from your property are reflected on your tax return. Both are reported on your K-1 tax form. Your K-1 legally represents your ownership of the business entity that purchased the apartment complex. In reality, we don't own the real estate. We own the legal business entity that owns the real estate. LLCs and LPs are the most common legal entity structures used in real estate.

VC Barcelona LLC is the legal entity that owned Barcelona Apartments. Barcelona Apartments is like any other business and is generating income and expenses, and like any other company, it has to report these business activities to the IRS every year. We do this by completing a Form 1065 Partnership Tax Return. We take the financial statements for that year, make a few tax adjustments, and then fill in the Form 1065 Partnership Tax Return and send it to the IRS.

Now, because we are using an LLC structure and we elected to file a Partnership Tax Return, the business entity does not pay taxes to the IRS. They simply file the Partnership Tax Return and issue the K-1s to the individual investors. The individual investors must include the K-1 in their personal tax return and pay any taxes.

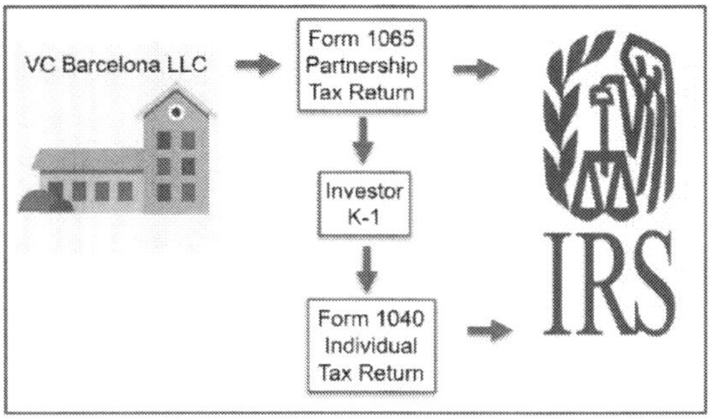

Before we dive into the specifics of one of my K-1s, let's establish a helpful analogy to grasp the larger context. Think of your K-1 in a similar manner as your W-2. Each year, your W-2 tax form provides the IRS with information about the money you earned from your job. Similarly, your K-1 tax form reports the money you made from real estate investments to the IRS annually.

Now, let's examine two of my actual K-1s from Barcelona Apartments. You can download a copy of my K-1s at www.curtishaines.com. The address and tax identification numbers have been changed for privacy.

Schedule K-1 (Form 1065) — **2011**

Department of the Treasury
Internal Revenue Service

For calendar year 2011, or tax year beginning ______ ending ______

Partner's Share of Income, Deductions, Credits, etc. ▶ See separate instructions.

☐ Final K-1 ☐ Amended K-1 OMB No. 1545-0099

Part I Information About the Partnership

A Partnership's employer identification number
26-4804816

B Partnership's name, address, city, state, and ZIP code
VC BARCELONA LLC
2801 Waterwall Dr
Houston, TX 77056

C IRS Center where partnership filed return
OGDEN, UT

D ☐ Check if this is a publicly traded partnership (PTP)

Part II Information About the Partner

E Partner's identifying number
987-56-4321

F Partner's name, address, city, state, and ZIP code
Curtis Haines
100 Carnarvon Drive
Houston, Tx 77024

G [X] General partner or LLC member-manager ☐ Limited partner or other LLC member

H [X] Domestic partner ☐ Foreign partner

I What type of entity is this partner? INDIVIDUAL

J Partner's share of profit, loss, and capital:

	Beginning	Ending
Profit	25.7500000%	25.7500000%
Loss	25.7500000%	25.7500000%
Capital	25.7500000%	25.7500000%

K Partner's share of liabilities at year end:

Nonrecourse	$ 34,889.
Qualified nonrecourse financing	$ 925,600.
Recourse	$ 0.

L Partner's capital account analysis:

Beginning capital account	$ 402,646.
Capital contributed during the year	$
Current year increase (decrease)	$ -52,815.
Withdrawals & distributions	$(245,589.)
Ending capital account	$ 104,242.

☐ Tax basis ☐ GAAP ☐ Section 704(b) book
[X] Other (explain) SEE STATEMENT

M Did the partner contribute property with a built-in gain or loss?
☐ Yes [X] No
If "Yes", attach statement (see instructions)

Part III Partner's Share of Current Year Income, Deductions, Credits, and Other Items

1 Ordinary business income (loss)		0.
2 Net rental real estate income (loss)		-42,360.
3 Other net rental income (loss)		
4 Guaranteed payments		
5 Interest income		180.
6a Ordinary dividends		
6b Qualified dividends		
7 Royalties		
8 Net short-term capital gain (loss)		
9a Net long-term capital gain (loss)		
9b Collectibles (28%) gain (loss)		
9c Unrecaptured sec 1250 gain		
10 Net section 1231 gain (loss)		
11 Other income (loss)		
12 Section 179 deduction		
13 Other deductions		
14 Self-employment earnings (loss)	A	0.
15 Credits		
16 Foreign transactions		
17 Alternative min tax (AMT) items	A	3,098.
18 Tax-exempt income and nondeductible expenses		
19 Distributions	A	245,589.
20 Other information	A	180.

*See attached statement for additional information.

For IRS Use Only

Schedule K-1 (Form 1065) **2013**

Department of the Treasury
Internal Revenue Service

For calendar year 2013, or tax year beginning ________ ending ________

Partner's Share of Income, Deductions, Credits, etc. ▶ See separate instructions.

[X] Final K-1 [ ] Amended K-1 OMB No. 1545-0099

Part I Information About the Partnership

A Partnership's employer identification number
26-4804816

B Partnership's name, address, city, state, and ZIP code
VC BARCELONA LLC
2801 Waterwall Dr
Houston, TX 77056

C IRS Center where partnership filed return
E-FILE

D [ ] Check if this is a publicly traded partnership (PTP)

Part II Information About the Partner

E Partner's identifying number
981-65-4321

F Partner's name, address, city, state, and ZIP code
Curtis Haines
100 Carnarvon Drive
Houston, Tx 77024

G [X] General partner or LLC member-manager [ ] Limited partner or other LLC member

H [X] Domestic partner [ ] Foreign partner

I1 What type of entity is this partner? INDIVIDUAL

I2 If this partner is a retirement plan (IRA/SEP/Keogh/etc.), check here [ ]

J Partner's share of profit, loss, and capital:

	Beginning	Ending
Profit	25.7500000%	25.7500000%
Loss	25.7500000%	25.7500000%
Capital	25.7500000%	25.7500000%

K Partner's share of liabilities at year end:

Nonrecourse	$	11,104.
Qualified nonrecourse financing	$	
Recourse	$	0.

L Partner's capital account analysis:

Beginning capital account	$	64,199.
Capital contributed during the year	$	
Current year increase (decrease)	$	784,167.
Withdrawals & distributions	$(	801,424.)
Ending capital account	$	46,942.

[ ] Tax basis [ ] GAAP [ ] Section 704(b) book
[X] Other (explain) SEE STATEMENT

M Did the partner contribute property with a built-in gain or loss?
[ ] Yes [X] No
If "Yes", attach statement (see instructions)

Part III Partner's Share of Current Year Income, Deductions, Credits, and Other Items

1 Ordinary business income (loss)	0.
2 Net rental real estate income (loss)	-7,544.
3 Other net rental income (loss)	
4 Guaranteed payments	
5 Interest income	26.
6a Ordinary dividends	
6b Qualified dividends	
7 Royalties	
8 Net short-term capital gain (loss)	
9a Net long-term capital gain (loss)	
9b Collectibles (28%) gain (loss)	
9c Unrecaptured sec 1250 gain	117,715.
10 Net section 1231 gain (loss)	793,694.
11 Other income (loss)	
12 Section 179 deduction	
13 Other deductions	
14 Self-employment earnings (loss)	A 0.
15 Credits	
16 Foreign transactions	
17 Alternative min tax (AMT) items	A -4,301. B* -10,086.
18 Tax-exempt income and nondeductible expenses	C* 18.
19 Distributions	A 801,424.
20 Other information	A 26.

*See attached statement for additional information.

For IRS Use Only

Let's start with the 2011 K-1. Take a look at box B, the partnership's name. You will see the name VC Barcelona LLC. Barcelona Apartments is owned by the legal entity named VC Barcelona LLC.

B Partnership's name, address, city, state, and ZIP code

VC BARCELONA LLC
2801 Waterwall Dr
Houston, TX 77056

Now take a look at box J, partner's share of profit, loss, and capital. You will see 25.75%. My ownership share in this entity is 25.75%.

J Partner's share of profit, loss, and capital:

	Beginning	Ending
Profit	25.7500000%	25.7500000%
Loss	25.7500000%	25.7500000%
Capital	25.7500000%	25.7500000%

Now look at box 2, Net rental real estate income (loss). The property's income and expenses are reported here in box 2. You will see a negative $42,360. This represents my share of the property's income and expenses. Box 2 determines how much net income from the apartment will be subject to taxation by the IRS.

2 Net rental real estate income (loss)

-42,360.

What if I told you Barcelona Apartments was one of my more successful properties? How can a thriving business with high rents and normal operating expenses report a loss? It's due to a tax deduction called depreciation. Don't worry about the details of the depreciation calculations; just understand that this tax calculation reduces the business income generated from your property, which is why most of our distributions are tax-free.

Now take a look at box 19 distributions. You will see $245,589. This represents my share of the property's cash distributions. Keep in mind that box 19 distributions also help the IRS track how much cash you receive from the business.

19 Distributions	
A	245,589.

Typically, the business will distribute cash flow from operations quarterly. In this particular year, I received distributions from cash flow from operations and cash-out refinancing. Approximately $50,000 came from cash flow from operations, while $195,000 came from a cash-out refinance. The total distributions received amounted to $245,589, which I deposited into my bank account. How much of this $245,589 cash is taxable? Remember, the IRS looks at box 2 to determine the taxable amount. Since there was a negative $42,360 on box 2, I didn't have to pay any taxes on the $245,589 cash distributions received.

Over the past 15 years, I have experienced 30 of these equity-capturing cash-out refinances. Every distribution I received from my apartments was reinvested in another property, and because those distributions were tax-free, I could accelerate my wealth-building. Consider how much taxes eat away at your reinvested dollars.

For example, let's say you receive a $100,000 cash-out refinance and invest it in another property that generates a 10% return over the next five years. At the end of five years, you would have $150,000. But if that $100,000 distribution was taxable, and you invested it in the exact same property, how much would you have after five years? Assuming a 33% tax rate, you would have about $100,000. In other words, it would take you five years just to break even and recoup what you gave to the IRS. Alternatively, by utilizing tax-free distributions, you would have 50% more funds available for reinvestment.

	$100,000	$67,000
Year 1	10,000	6,700
Year 2	10,000	6,700
Year 3	10,000	6,700
Year 4	10,000	6,700
Year 5	10,000	6,700
	$150,000	$100,500

Now, let's discuss what happens when you sell a property. In 2013, I sold Barcelona Apartments. Looking at box 19 from my 2013 K-1, you'll see that I received $801,424 in distributions, which I deposited into my bank account.

19 Distributions	
A	801,424.

How much of that was subject to taxes? When you sell a property, the IRS looks at boxes 9 and 10 to calculate your taxes on the sale. Looking at my 2013 K-1, you will see $117,715 in box 9 and $793,694 in box 10.

9c Unrecaptured sec 1250 gain	
	117,715.
10 Net section 1231 gain (loss)	
	793,694.

This represents my share of the gain from the sale, totaling $911,409 (117,715+793,694). The average tax rate for this gain was around 20%. If Barcelona Apartments was your only property as a sole owner, and you didn't engage in a 1031 exchange, you would have to pay approximately $182,281 in taxes (20% tax rate X 911,409 gain). However, by utilizing a 1031 exchange, you can avoid paying any taxes. Furthermore, if you are an active buyer like me, you will likely have enough loss carryforward to offset some or all of the gains from the sale.

Remember the $42,360 loss on box 2 in 2011? Imagine if you had 10 or 20 properties generating similar losses year after year. What happens when you can't utilize those losses? They get carried forward to the next year and the following years. Consequently, I had enough loss carryforward to offset the gains, resulting in no taxes being paid on this sale. In fact, I sold eight more properties with large gains shortly after this one and paid no taxes.

If you are a passive investor with only a few passive investments, you are unlikely to have enough loss carryforward to offset all of your gains. Paying taxes is not necessarily a bad thing. I had an unusually high number of dispositions in 2022 and started to pay capital gains taxes. I'm okay with that, and you should be too. I simply prefer to postpone it for as long as possible.

Returning to the W-2 analogy, let's consider how many additional W-2 jobs one can undertake daily. If you work a full-time job, it might be possible to fit in one other part-time job. However, due to the limited number of hours a day, our earned income is directly linked to the time we invest. Now, let's shift our focus to K-1s. How many K-1s can generate cash flow on any given day? The answer is limitless. Unlike active income earned through trading our time, passive income generated through K-1s is not constrained by the number of hours in a day.

Reinvesting Tax-Deferred Funds

I want to emphasize the concept of tax-free distributions. Let's examine the compounding effect of reinvesting tax-free funds. Most of us understand the power of compounding interest but fail to grasp the impact of taxes on our long-term investments.

Numerous examples illustrate the effects of taxes on investments, but my favorite one goes like this: Imagine you invest $1 and double your money every year for the next 20 years. After the first year, you have $2; after the second year, $4; after the third year, $8; and so on. By the end of 20 years, you will have accumulated $1,048,576. That's the power of compounding. So, what happens when we consider taxes in the same scenario? Take a guess. If you're fortunate enough to pay only 34% in taxes yearly, how much do you think your dollar would have grown in 20 years after taxes? Would it be around $750,000? Maybe even $500,000?

Would it be reasonable to have half of your money go towards paying taxes? Assuming you have an average annual tax rate of 34%, at the end of those same 20 years, your net amount would be just over $47,000. Yes, you read that correctly—$47,000! That's a difference of over $1 million compared to the tax-free scenario.

Please stop for a moment and contemplate what you just read. This should help you see the sleight of hand magic trick I alluded to at the beginning of this chapter.

High-net-worth families recognized this concept generations ago. The example I just provided covered a 20-year period, but can you imagine the wealth that high-net-worth families can build over several generations?

Now you can understand why real estate investment is so appealing to them. For most of us, the idea of buying an apartment complex may seem daunting. Investing in apartments was never part of our everyday conversations at home. However, high-net-worth families have been doing it for generations, and it's as normal to them as it is for the average person to open a savings account or start a 401(k).

Thanks to Del, the idea of buying apartments is now a topic of discussion at my family's dinner table. Moreover, thanks to Del, most people I associate with own multiple apartments. For the first time, average individuals like you and me have the opportunity to invest just like high-net-worth families. This kind of investing wasn't readily available to the middle class until now. We can bring together a group of middle-class families to generate enough buying power to acquire large properties or individually invest in smaller properties. Either way, we can enjoy some of the same tax benefits that high-net-worth families have benefited from for generations. How amazing is that?

Chapter 10

The Family Office

I hope my story inspires you to start your family office. It doesn't matter your net worth or where I am catching you in life. It is more about changing your mindset and making business decisions about your assets. As I share my story about the family office, I get lots of questions about the details of actually running a family office. Let me be very clear. I am not an expert in this area. It is more important to get the overall concepts and less important about the details.

The first main hurdle would be for you to reach financial independence. Once you hit that milestone, you can take your family office to the next level and get into the details of running a family office. Before sharing how I run my family office with you, let's cover the basics.

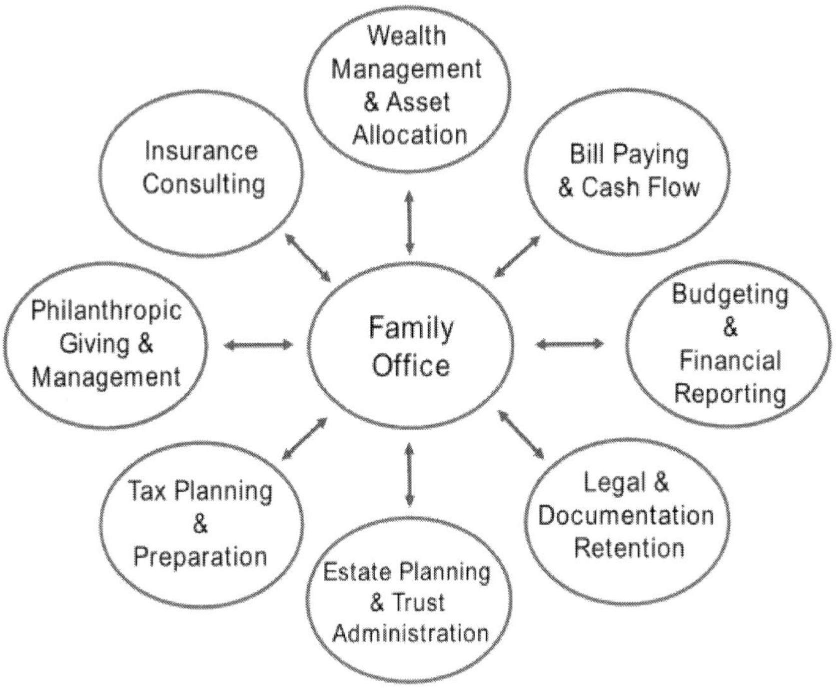

Overview of a Family Office

Over the past decade, family offices have become increasingly popular due to the accumulation of wealth by high-net-worth families and the desire for more personalized financial management solutions. A family office is a private wealth management organization that serves high-net-worth individuals or families. It provides a range of services to manage the financial affairs and investments of the family to preserve and grow their wealth over generations. Affluent families typically establish family offices to centralize the management of their assets, streamline financial operations, and address various needs, such as estate planning, tax optimization, and philanthropy.

Here are some key aspects and features of family offices:

- Structure: Family offices can be structured in different ways, depending on the needs and preferences of the family. They can be single-family offices (SFOs), serving only one wealthy family, or multifamily offices (MFOs), which provide services to multiple affluent families. Some families establish their own independent family office, while others work with established financial institutions or specialized firms that offer family office services.

- Wealth Management and Asset Allocation: Family offices offer comprehensive wealth management services, including investment management, financial planning, risk management, and estate planning. They work closely with the family to develop customized investment strategies, aligning them with the family's goals, risk tolerance, and values. The investment portfolio may include a diverse range of assets, such as stocks, bonds, real estate, private equity, hedge funds, and alternative investments. By diversifying across various asset classes, family offices seek to achieve a balance between potential growth and risk mitigation, aiming to generate long-term wealth and preserve capital.

- Bill Paying and Cash Flow: Family offices streamline financial operations by managing bill paying and cash flow. They handle day-to-day financial transactions, ensuring that bills, expenses, and other financial obligations are paid accurately and in a timely manner. Family offices maintain detailed records of income and expenses, enabling the family to clearly understand their cash flow and ensuring that liquidity needs are met effectively.

- Budgeting and Financial Reporting: Family offices assist in creating and maintaining budgets. They work closely with the family to develop realistic and sustainable budgets that align with their financial goals and lifestyle choices. Family offices also provide regular financial reporting and consolidation services, giving the family a clear overview of their assets, liabilities, income, and expenses. This involves accounting, bookkeeping, and preparing financial statements. Family offices help families monitor their financial performance and make informed decisions by maintaining accurate records and providing transparent reporting.

- Legal and Documentation Retention: Family offices ensure that important legal and financial documents are properly organized and retained. They work closely with the family to establish efficient systems for document management, including wills, trusts, contracts, and other legal agreements. Family offices oversee the safekeeping of these documents, maintaining an organized record-keeping system to ensure easy access and retrieval when needed.

- Estate Planning and Trust Administration: Family offices play a crucial role in estate planning and trust administration. They work with the family and their legal advisors to develop comprehensive estate plans, taking into consideration tax implications, wealth transfer strategies, and philanthropic objectives. Family offices assist in setting up and administering trusts, ensuring that assets are protected and transferred according to the family's wishes. They also coordinate with attorneys, accountants, and other professionals to ensure proper estate administration and minimize potential conflicts or issues.

- Tax Planning and Preparation: Family offices assist with tax planning and preparation strategies to minimize tax liabilities while ensuring compliance with applicable laws and regulations. They work with tax experts and legal advisors to identify tax-efficient structures, manage complex tax issues, and optimize the family's tax position. This can include tax planning for investments, business operations, cross-border transactions, and estate planning.

- Philanthropic Giving and Management: Many family offices support the family's philanthropic endeavors by facilitating charitable giving and impact investing. They help families define their philanthropic goals, establish charitable foundations or trusts, and manage donations. Family offices may also assist in identifying and evaluating impact investment opportunities that align with the family's values and social or environmental objectives.

- Insurance Consulting: Family offices provide insurance consulting services to help the family protect their assets and mitigate risks. They assess the family's insurance needs and work with insurance brokers to identify appropriate coverage options. Family offices review existing insurance policies, ensuring they are up to date and adequately cover the family's assets and liabilities. They also manage claims and liaise with insurance providers to ensure the family receives fair and timely settlements.

- Lifestyle Management: Besides financial matters, family offices can assist with various lifestyle management services. These include concierge services, travel planning, property management, art collection management, and coordination of personal staff, such as household staff, security personnel, and advisors in areas like health and wellness.

- Governance and Succession Planning: Family offices often play a crucial role in governance and succession planning. They help the family establish structures and processes for decision-making, wealth transfer, and the continuity of the family's legacy. This may involve developing family constitutions, setting up family councils, educating the next generation about wealth management, and facilitating communication and collaboration among family members.

Overall, family offices provide a holistic approach to wealth management, integrating financial expertise, specialized services, and personalized support to meet the unique needs of affluent families. Their primary objective is to preserve and enhance the family's wealth while addressing various aspects of their financial and non-financial affairs.

My Family Office

Now that we have a general understanding of the structure of a family office, let me share what I personally do with my family office.

Wealth Management and Asset Allocation: Most of my time is dedicated to this part of my family office. That will more than likely change over time. In my investment portfolio, around 80% is allocated to real estate, while the remaining 20% is in cash or cash equivalents. I am required to maintain a minimum of 5% liquid assets per my loan covenants. During the peak of my acquisitions, when I played the 30-day rule game, I did fall below my minimum in a month or two but always met my quarterly reporting requirements. I moved 5% of my liquid assets to a financial advisor to help me maintain my required liquidity. Basically, he knows I can't touch those funds.

In 2023, I stopped playing the 30-day rule game for various reasons. I am now stacking cash to prepare for the next cycle, which is why my liquid assets are higher than normal. I have a long-term bullish outlook on real estate and will continue reinvesting my funds in multifamily real estate. Around 80% of my real estate portfolio is located in Texas, with the remaining 20% outside of Texas.

I closely monitor all my real estate investments using a customized spreadsheet centered around the schedule of real estate form (SREO), which lenders require me to update according to loan covenants. You can download a standard SREO template at www.curtishaines.com. I have set up automated alerts for specific criteria, such as occupancy, debt service coverage ratio, loan maturity, net operating income, expense ratio, and distributions.

I also use the same customized spreadsheet to track my return on equity for individual properties. When my return on equity falls below a certain threshold, I will start planning the appropriate exit strategy to capture the equity gains: Sell to capture 100% of the equity gains or refinance to capture a nice chunk of the equity gains. I review potential real estate investments on a weekly basis.

Bill Paying and Cash Flow: To streamline the process, I have set up auto-pay for all our bills and auto-deposit for most of our cash flow. I avoid using checks or cash for payments, and if necessary, I utilize alternative payment apps like Zelle or Venmo. Automation minimizes the time spent on day-to-day financial transactions and ensures bills, expenses, and other financial obligations are paid accurately and in a timely manner.

I use Quicken software to manage most financial tasks and run basic reports to monitor our cash flow and liquidity needs. Our monthly expenses are covered by a basic checking account, which I keep at a maximum of three months' worth of expenses, reducing the risk of loss in case of a compromised bank account. Automated alerts notify me when the funds need replenishing. I track partner distributions using the same SREO spreadsheet and set automatic alerts for any discrepancies.

Budgeting and Financial Reporting: I rely on Quicken software for budgeting and financial reporting. While in the past, I used budgeting to save money; my current focus is on monitoring our cash flow from a distance. I set up our annual budget based on historical trends and run saved reports to identify any areas requiring special attention. For example, I am not as concerned about the details of each category unless it has broken through a historical trend. That historical trend is set with a budgeted number. I also use budgets to track my other businesses from a distance.

Quicken software also does a good job tracking our net worth and makes it easy for me to update my personal financial statement quarterly per lender requirements. As mentioned earlier, it is very important that you track your net worth and return on net worth annually to determine how good of a job you are doing as CEO of your family office. Analyzing your CEO scorecard will help you make timely course corrections as needed.

Legal and Documentation Retention: I consult a real estate attorney to handle commercial contracts related to my investments. When forming partnerships to invest in real estate, I engage an SEC attorney. Additionally, I have an estate attorney for estate planning and asset protection and a general attorney for significant matters requiring my signature. I ensure that a legal professional reviews all my documents before I sign them.

Document retention is managed using Google Drive, where electronic copies are stored. Most paper documents are scanned and shredded, while sensitive original documents are kept in a safe deposit box after being scanned.

Estate Planning and Trust Administration: We have established three customized trusts aligned with our family's specific goals. I recommend seeking a referral from your CPA for an estate attorney and ensuring a close working relationship between the estate attorney and CPA to optimize protection and minimize potential tax-related issues. If they are not familiar with each other, involving your CPA in meetings with the estate attorney is advisable.

Don't set up a trust just to set up a trust. It needs to be customized to your family's needs and goals. Don't set it up too early. Trusts add an extra layer of complexity and expense. Obviously, don't set up trusts too late in life. You will need enough time to plan and optimize asset protection properly.

Tax Planning and Preparation: A CPA who specializes in real estate handles our tax planning and preparation. They help us leverage all the tax benefits associated with real estate investments, as discussed in chapter six. This CPA manages our individual and business tax returns and has collaborated effectively with the estate attorney. Recognizing the critical roles played by legal and tax professionals, I prioritize their expertise and willingly pay top dollar for their services.

Insurance Consulting: We work directly with our insurance brokers to identify appropriate coverage options and always get a second opinion every other year. We ensure our investment properties are covered by property and liability insurance. Additionally, we hold umbrella liability insurance for our family, along with standard home, car, health, and life insurance. A $5 million umbrella liability insurance is relatively inexpensive and usually obtained through your homeowner's insurance policy. Estate planning plays a significant role in protecting most of our personal assets.

Philanthropic Giving and Management: We have set up auto-pay for most of our contributions to our church and other charities. Apart from scheduled donations, we prefer to make anonymous contributions to individuals or organizations close to us, including random acts of kindness.

As you can see, outsourcing various key areas of the family office to professionals is easily achievable. However, the knowledge and experience I have gained through Lifestyles Unlimited enable me to handle wealth management independently. I do not require a team of analysts to review potential investments. My accounting background allows me to manage financial responsibilities in-house.

If accounting is not your strength, I recommend learning the basics. When your operations are small, it is unwise to entrust your finances entirely to someone else. Small businesses lack the internal controls present in larger enterprises, putting them at risk if only one person manages the books. With most of my family office tasks automated, I am only averaging about two hours a week working in the family office business. The majority of my time is spent working on the business of real estate.

The Next Generation

In the near future, I plan to expand my family office team by adding a new employee. I strongly believe in involving the entire family in the business of running my family office.

The other day, my five-year-old daughter asked me, "What does Mommy do?" I happily replied, "Mommy is a music teacher." Then came her curious gaze toward me, and she asked, "And what about you, Daddy?" I replied, "I help people buy properties," proudly pointing to an apartment within our sight. I couldn't resist adding, "And one day, you could take over Daddy's real estate business," But, to my surprise, she quickly responded, "No, I want to play music like Mommy." Given her mother's musical talent, it seems unlikely I'll win her over, but if she wants to play music, I'll cheer her on just like my parents did for me.

Nevertheless, I believe it's essential for her to grasp the language of business, as it is crucial for the continued success of our family office. The language of business holds equal importance to fundamental skills like reading, writing, and math. It is the key to understanding a business's financial health and performance, effectively communicating its well-being and financial status.

In particular, accounting stands as the primary language of business. With a solid understanding of accounting, she will confidently navigate the complexities of the business world. This valuable skill set will enable her to interpret financial reports, evaluate profitability, assess risks, and identify growth opportunities.

Acquiring proficiency in the language of business will contribute to the success of our family office and prepare her to excel in various professional fields, whether as an entrepreneur, executive, investor, or musician.

I would like to emphasize one last thing regarding the family office. It is important to maintain a clear distinction between the day-to-day operations of your family office and the day-to-day operations of your real estate business. These are separate business entities, and avoiding commingling funds or sharing the same back-office team between them is essential.

My journey in real estate has been extraordinary, primarily shaped by the invaluable guidance and support I received from Lifestyles Unlimited. Joining this group has proven to be one of the most pivotal choices of my life. Through their expertise, mentorship, and steadfast commitment to their members' success, Lifestyles Unlimited has opened doors and transformed dreams into realities.

In the remaining chapters, I will share some valuable lessons I have learned by exploring in more detail some of the stories I covered earlier. Life presents obstacles that can halt our progress and force us to take a new path. I will delve deeper into how I overcame the fallout from the 2008 economic downturn and my battle with cancer. I will also provide more insight into my personal life and how it has influenced my real estate journey.

Finally, I will touch on my current role as a mentor in the multifamily real estate industry and how I use my experiences to guide others on their paths to success. I hope my extended personal narrative provides a deeper understanding of my journey to creating wealth, provides some life wisdom that will help you lead a richer life, and inspires you to push through adversity and pursue your dreams.

Chapter 11

How I Lost $2 Million in 2 Months

I used to believe that the key to achieving financial success was obtaining a good education and securing a well-paying job. Pursuing this goal, I worked two part-time jobs while attending college full-time. Although school was always a challenge, I put in the extra effort and graduated with honors, ultimately landing my dream job at one of the country's largest accounting firms. I was on track for a successful career, with aspirations of becoming a partner in a prestigious international accounting firm.

A Difficult Career Change

However, after a couple of years of grueling work weeks and spending countless hours on tax preparation, I came to two realizations.

Firstly, I was not good at my job, no matter how hard I worked. Secondly, I noticed that my superiors, including my boss and their boss, were exerting as much effort as I did. Suddenly, the prospect of reaching the esteemed position of a partner lost its allure.

This led me to make a career change, transitioning into sales. I quickly discovered that I wasn't suited for sales due to my introverted nature. I was more comfortable working with numbers, spreadsheets and being a behind-the-scenes worker. Thinking I could excel in sales after relocating to a new city seemed to be a misguided decision. Moreover, the sales job was commission-based, and I had a three-month timeframe to prove my worth; otherwise I faced termination. These were crucial details that I failed to consider, as the potential monetary rewards primarily enticed me.

Unknown to me then, upper management had contemplated letting me go multiple times within the initial nine months of my employment due to poor sales performance. My former boss, affectionately referred to as "PK," took a bold stance and trusted me despite the disappointing outcomes. It was through his unwavering support that I secured my very first sale as a recruiter. His influence on my life left an indelible mark on my heart, and I will forever hold a special place for him.

Thanks to PK's exceptional leadership, I eventually became one of the company's top recruiters. What I lacked in skills, I made up for with hard work. Unlike my previous accounting job, the more effort I put into sales, the more money I earned. What perplexed me at the time was that even with the increased income, I still found it challenging to make ends meet. Although my initial plan of attending school to secure a good job had somewhat worked out, I was far from feeling financially successful.

For the next 14 years, I dedicated my career to the staffing industry as a recruiter, assisting accounting professionals in finding suitable employment. Eventually, I joined forces with two partners and started a new company. Initially, we were equal partners, but when my partners decided to get married, I suddenly became a minority owner overnight. Although we faced challenges in the early years, we managed to grow the staffing firm into a highly successful business, earning accolades such as being named among the Inc. 500 fastest-growing companies, the top 10 best places to work, and the top 25 recruiting firms.

Unfortunately, four years later, my partners' marriage fell apart, and the business became the kids in their divorce. The only viable solution was selling the company to settle the custody battle.

My share of the proceeds from the business sale was just over $2.1 million. It seemed like a substantial amount of money at that time, but I knew it wouldn't be enough to retire comfortably. My average annual income had exceeded $200,000 throughout my career as a recruiter. Despite earning a six-figure salary, I still found myself living paycheck to paycheck. Considering my current expenditure, basic calculations suggest that the funds would last around 10 years.

Moreover, retirement wasn't something I desired. Spending such a significant amount of time doing one thing becomes ingrained in your identity. My world revolved around recruiting, and our company was on the verge of exponential growth. We had an exceptional team and were expanding into other specialized areas within the recruiting industry. We had already expanded our office space multiple times and were negotiating a new lease to double our footprint. Amidst all this, I experienced a whirlwind of emotions, primarily a profound sense of loss.

The 2008 Financial Crisis

I deposited the funds into my bank account, and the following day, I transferred them to TD Ameritrade in search of some yield while I contemplated my next steps. The best option seemed to be a sweep account that would automatically invest the funds in a mutual fund named the Reserve Fund. I was assured that my funds would be secure. However, just two months later, the 2008 financial crisis, also known as the global financial crisis or the Great Recession, struck. It was an immense economic downturn with severe consequences, the most significant financial crisis in the United States since the Great Depression of the 1930s.

The crisis was triggered by the collapse of the United States housing market, fueled by a combination of low interest rates, easy credit access, and the prevalence of subprime mortgage lending. Subprime mortgages were loans given to individuals with poor credit history. These mortgages were bundled into complex financial products called mortgage-backed securities (MBS) and collateralized debt obligations (CDOs), falsely rated as safe investments by credit rating agencies, despite their high risk.

As housing prices began to decline, many borrowers defaulted on their subprime mortgages, leading to a wave of foreclosures. This created a downward spiral, causing housing prices to drop further and leading to significant losses for financial institutions holding mortgage-backed securities. Financial institutions had engaged in risky behavior, including excessive leverage and complex derivatives, which amplified the impact of the crisis. The securitization of mortgages and the interconnectedness of global financial markets allowed the crisis to spread rapidly.

The crisis escalated with the collapse of Lehman Brothers, a prominent investment bank. In September 2008, Lehman Brothers filed for bankruptcy. It was the largest bankruptcy filing in U.S. history and sent shockwaves through the global financial system, eroding confidence and triggering widespread financial panic. Many financial institutions and investors held Lehman Brothers' bonds in their portfolios. Stock markets around the world plummeted, erasing trillions of dollars in wealth. Investor confidence was severely shaken, leading to a prolonged period of market volatility.

The Reserve Fund

The Reserve Fund, the mutual fund holding all of my money, had invested significant assets in Lehman Brothers' debt securities, including commercial paper and medium-term notes. These holdings were considered safe and highly liquid, but when Lehman Brothers collapsed, their value plummeted, causing significant losses for the Reserve Fund. The Lehman Brothers' bankruptcy triggered a crisis in the money market industry because money market funds, including the Reserve Fund, held Lehman Brothers' debt securities that suddenly became nearly worthless. The Reserve Fund "broke the buck," which means its net asset value (NAV) fell below $1 per share. This was a rare occurrence for money market funds, which are generally expected to maintain a stable NAV.

Although my funds represented only a fraction of the trillions of dollars lost during the crisis, it wasn't just about the amount; it was the gut-wrenching feeling of losing everything I had worked tirelessly to build—my company, my savings, and now, my shattered dreams of rebuilding. It all slipped away, leaving me with nothing.

It's undeniable that a substantial portion of the populace felt its direct impact. With the U.S. unemployment rate soaring to a peak of 10%, countless individuals found themselves jobless as a direct consequence of the crisis. Foreclosures surged by 81% from the previous year, totaling about 3.1 million in 2008. Many saw their nest eggs evaporate due to the stock market's plunge.

Now, amidst all these events, I found myself entangled in what undoubtedly became one of the most pivotal transactions of my life. I was under contract to purchase a 176-unit apartment, and shortly after starting the closing process, I lost all of my funds. The temptation to abandon real estate was strong, as the risks extended far beyond losing my savings. The possibility of breaching the purchase contract loomed, which would have entailed more substantial financial and legal consequences.

Just when things seemed dire, my mentor came to my rescue, assuming control of the purchase contract and relieving me of any additional burdens and legal troubles. Del pulled together a partnership with several families, successfully closing the deal. To my astonishment, he even included me in this partnership, converting my sunk costs into valuable equity.

As I previously mentioned, Del was an aggressive buyer during this tumultuous period. The 176-unit apartment was one of five properties he scooped up in the wake of the 2008 market crash. His actions mirrored his advice to his members—to buy amidst the chaos. And true to form, Del distributed millions in profits years later to the families that joined those partnerships. His guidance and actions undoubtedly shaped my path toward success in real estate.

Witnessing Del's astute maneuvers during this period gave me a firsthand glimpse into the strategies of a truly successful individual. This experience made it easier for me to purchase my first two properties on credit using my margin account.

After my first two real estate acquisitions, I stopped actively keeping track of updates about the Reserve Fund. Based on all the updates at that time, there was little hope of any recovery of funds. Besides, I had something positive to focus on. I knew these two properties would help me repay the margin balance and establish a secure future for my family.

The frequency of email updates about the Reserve Fund decreased significantly, and I would only receive one or two updates every quarter. Over time, as months passed by, I gradually came to terms with my losses and moved forward.

To my pleasant surprise, 18 months later, I unexpectedly received half of the funds I had lost. Over the next ten years, I gradually received small incremental payments stemming from the Lehman Brothers' bankruptcy. Finally, after a decade had passed, I received the last payment, ultimately recovering approximately 75 cents on the dollar.

It's quite remarkable how things turned out even more favorably than initially expected. I avoided partnerships to buy one apartment and ended up embracing partnerships and buying 187 apartments. Who would have thought losing $2 million in two months would have been a good thing? It serves as yet another instance of a hidden blessing. Just as one door closes, another one opens.

The Current Market

Before proceeding to the next chapter, we must address the current economic environment. As previously discussed, I've deliberately scaled back my real estate acquisitions due to multiple considerations. The primary concern is the potential impact of surging interest rates on the real estate sector and the broader economy. There's consensus among many macroeconomists that we are currently navigating a period of profound uncertainty. Drawing from the insights of various experts I've closely followed, I anticipate a significant market correction, likely within the next 18 to 24 months. My prediction falls around the end of 2024 or the beginning of 2025. This market adjustment could potentially surpass the severity of the 2008 financial crisis.

However, this scenario might present a prime investment opportunity for newcomers to the real estate field. Now is the time to do the work needed to be prepared for the next real estate cycle. You don't want to start in the middle of an upswing.

As for experienced property owners, our current strategy involves offloading properties with variable-rate loans while maintaining a long-term hold on properties secured with fixed-rate loans. The lion's share of my portfolio is indeed anchored by fixed-rate loans. I've already successfully divested from several properties under variable-rate loans, with plans underway to dispose of the remaining few. Looking ahead, I maintain a strongly optimistic stance on the long-term prospects of real estate.

Chapter 12

My Battle with Cancer

I spent three years battling stage three colorectal cancer. At 45 years old, my first colonoscopy was still five years away, and there was no family history of cancer. I had never undergone any surgeries, nor did I have any prior health issues. Moreover, I didn't drink or smoke, and my active lifestyle, including competitive sports, had me in better physical shape at 45 than during high school.

Denial

Initially, I struggled to come to terms with the reality of my situation, uncertain about what the upcoming years would hold. I assumed I could stay active in sports and keep up with my normal day-to-day activities. Perhaps this uncertainty and my desire to maintain a sense of normalcy led me to keep my diagnosis private. Alternatively, I may have been in denial, unwilling to confront the truth. Only my immediate family and key members of my third-party management company knew about my condition. Outwardly, I projected a positive and pragmatic demeanor regarding my diagnosis, but internally, fear overwhelmed me.

Throughout my journey, my wife became my unwavering support and rock. Her presence by my side every day was crucial to my ability to endure the treatments. She guided me through important decisions regarding hospitals, doctors, treatments, and procedures. When she asked if I wanted to know what lay ahead, I declined, fearing that the stress of anticipating the road ahead would be overwhelming. Instead, I focused on taking one day at a time. Looking back, I believe I made the right choice, as knowing what I know now, I question whether I could endure another round of treatments and surgeries.

Treatment and Recovery

Over those three years, I underwent two complete rounds of chemotherapy and radiation treatments, as well as two surgeries. As the first round of chemo and radiation progressed, the symptoms began to manifest, reaching their peak at the midpoint. The skin on my hands and feet peeled away completely, rendering walking and gripping objects incredibly painful. I remember the arduous task of typing emails and providing property updates as I painstakingly hunted and pecked on the keyboard. Other bodily changes occurred during that time, some more painful and too graphic to detail here.

While I had not been religious in the past, my battle with cancer led me to embrace Christianity wholeheartedly. In moments when I doubted my ability to endure the next treatment, I immersed myself in sermons and books by Timothy Keller and other inspirational thought leaders.

As I went through the ordeal of battling cancer, I found that the physical pain, though excruciating at first, gradually became more bearable as my body adapted to the treatments and medications. The doctors and family were always there to provide support and guidance, helping me cope with the physical challenges.

However, the emotional pain was an entirely different beast altogether. The uncertainty surrounding my survival weighed heavily on my mind and heart. Every day, I grappled with a whirlwind of emotions—fear, anxiety, and sadness—never knowing for sure what the outcome would be. It felt like walking on a tightrope between hope and despair, with every moment carrying the weight of life and death.

Throughout the journey, I had to learn to navigate the rollercoaster of emotions. There were days when I felt optimistic, believing that I could conquer anything, and then there were moments of doubt and despair, fearing the worst. It was a constant battle within myself, trying to stay positive while confronting the stark reality of my circumstances.

One particular appointment stands out in my memory when I was having a full-body scan to receive approval for the final surgery, a reversal ileostomy. We were initially elated and celebrated our positive outcome. However, halfway home, MD Anderson called and asked us to return urgently, revealing that something new had been found on the scan. Did the tumor grow? Did the cancer spread to other parts of my body? With no answers to our questions, we anxiously complied. The two-hour wait for another scan and the subsequent meeting with the doctor remains one of the lowest points in my life. Fortunately, it turned out to be a false positive, and I was cleared for surgery.

Silver Lining

Eventually, I found peace and began to envision a positive future. Yet, during those moments of despair, my mind dwelled on the regret of not having children. Despite being married for over twenty years, life's circumstances repeatedly hindered our plans to start a family. My wife's successful music career and frequent travels, along with my dedication to work, presented ongoing obstacles.

Medical experts had informed us that the probability of us becoming parents was less than 2%, given our age and the detrimental effects of chemotherapy and radiation on my body. Against all odds, our miracle baby arrived, bringing immeasurable joy to our lives. A happy, healthy, and beautiful baby girl graced us with her presence. Looking back, the experience of battling cancer unexpectedly brought a silver lining to our family's story. That might sound odd, but it was a wake-up call to start our family. And without a doubt, our baby girl is our most treasured gift.

Now, I enjoy the freedom to spend unlimited time with my family, unburdened by a job that once consumed my entire day. I can pursue my interests and manage my real estate and family office at my own pace. I continue to engage with real estate, not out of necessity but in genuine desire.

Approaching the 10-year mark, I have yet to recover fully, but I have reclaimed a semblance of a normal life. However, the multiple rounds of radiation, chemotherapy, and surgeries have left me with lasting side effects. Thankfully, my energy levels have improved, and the frequency of abdominal pains has lessened. Nonetheless, I must adhere to a strict diet and avoid most lunch and dinner invitations for health reasons. Due to my circumstances, I could not function in a traditional 9–5 corporate job. Fortunately, real estate gives me the freedom to work around my challenges.

Although I no longer participate in competitive sports, I've established a routine of strength training and cardio exercises four to five days a week to maintain my fitness. Additionally, I regularly consult with a nutritionist to ensure I maintain healthy eating habits.

Early Detection

Early detection is truly our best weapon in the fight against cancer. I recall the ominous feeling that something wasn't quite right for over a year before I was initially diagnosed with cancer—a mistake I'm determined not to repeat and one I sincerely hope no one else does, either.

Two years ago, I had another cancer scare and immediately opted for a GRAIL test and a follow-up colonoscopy. Much to my relief, the results for both tests were negative. Discussing the latest advancements in early cancer detection with your doctor is crucial.

In recent times, liquid biopsies have been making waves in the medical field. These tests analyze components like circulating tumor cells (CTCs), circulating tumor DNA (ctDNA), and other biomarkers found in the blood. They are proving to be a non-invasive way of detecting and tracking cancer in its early stages. These tests are capable of identifying genetic mutations and other changes related to cancer. GRAIL is at the forefront of this medical innovation, pioneering some of the most advanced liquid biopsy tests available today.

Visiting MD Anderson remains emotionally challenging, as I encounter countless others engaged in their own cancer battles, spanning across different age groups. If you find yourself feeling down, even if you're in good health, I highly recommend having lunch at MD

Anderson on a Tuesday. Their cafeteria rivals the size of food courts in the largest malls in America and offers an impressive selection of food. Unfortunately, it is also crowded, akin to the chaos of Black Friday shopping. By experiencing the profound effects of cancer firsthand and witnessing its impact on countless individuals, one can truly appreciate the wealth of good health.

Chapter 13

Letting Go of Day-to-Day Operations

Most of my time was spent working IN the business before real estate. Despite being an owner, I was still running a desk and working on daily back-office tasks. In our later years, we did hire a business consultant to help us grow. I never figured out how to work ON the business until real estate. Del Walmsley helped me finally get it. He would always joke about not having the keys to any of his businesses.

Working IN the Business

Many budding business owners fall into a similar trap.

A baker starting a bakery ends up baking all day, working IN the business. A plumber launching a plumbing company is caught up fixing toilets and sinks, also working IN the business. An accountant starts a staffing business; all he wants to do is the back-office accounting and payroll between sales calls. Just like them, I was working IN the business.

I am embarrassed to admit I was just as guilty on my first multifamily property. I found someone on Craigslist giving away their monkey grass for free, spent the whole weekend digging it up, and then replanted it along the walkway of our apartment; talk about getting entangled in the minutiae of my own business. For small property owners who can't afford full-time staff, doing some work on the property is reasonable and often enjoyable. But I had full-time staff and no excuse for my involvement.

In the beginning, I would pick up trash when I was walking around the property; that was someone else's job. I would climb the roof to trim back overhanging trees; that was someone else's job. I would do night checks to see if any lights needed to be replaced; that was someone else's job. I could go on and on about all the daily tasks I got myself into. Delegating was a muscle that needed to be worked on.

Another interesting thing about my first acquisition was that the lender forced me to outsource the property's operations to a third-party property management company. After the 2008 market collapse, lenders would no longer allow first-time owners to self-manage. I thought this was ridiculous at the time. My first property only had two employees. I was a successful business owner. My prior business had employed 20 times the number of people my property did, so I was confident I could easily manage just two employees. Besides, who in their right mind outsources their core business? Outsourcing back-office tasks, sure. But operations? I disagreed.

Thankfully, I found a third-party property management company willing to let me stay involved in the day-to-day operations. I could implement all the best practices I learned from Del. The property management company was very open to my input, and they shared with me all their standard operating procedures and training manuals. They allowed me to handle as many of the IN-the-business tasks as I wanted. Boy, was I eager to work IN the business at that time. I was very upfront with them, too. I assured them that our arrangement was temporary, intending to let them go and self-manage once I gained enough multifamily operations experience to satisfy my lender.

The third-party management company also managed my second acquisition per my lender's requirement. We continued to work together seamlessly and duplicated the same systems and procedures as we did on the first acquisition. I continued to work as a "manager in training," introducing myself to our residents as such and always referring to our onsite manager, typically in their early 20s, as my boss. It led to amusing interactions, including one resident wondering why I was still "in training" after two years. I didn't realize it at the time, but he had recently moved from my first property to my second property, and by this time, two years had passed. I can only guess he thought I was a slow learner.

Working ON the Business

On my third acquisition, the lender said I could now self-manage. By this time, I began to realize I added more value working ON the business than working IN the business. If I started my own property management company, I would be deep IN the business for a few more years. I made the easy decision to keep my third-party management company. As I grew my portfolio, I started delegating more and more of my daily IN-the-business tasks to my property supervisors.

When I got hit with cancer, I was forced to delegate 100% of my tasks. I was relieved I had them on my team, knowing my investors and properties would be in good hands while I battled cancer. The interesting part about letting go was that I never reclaimed any of those responsibilities after overcoming cancer. To this day, I am happy to say that I now spend all of my time working ON the business, and, much like Del Walmsley, I don't hold any keys to my businesses either.

Looking back, it took a life event like cancer to force me to let go of the last few IN-the-business tasks I so dearly wanted to hold on to. Why? It all stemmed from the belief system ingrained in me from an early age—my superpower was always "work harder."

I struggled with achieving good grades in school, so I committed myself to studying more diligently than many others. Sales skills didn't come naturally either, so I made up for it by investing more time and effort than my colleagues. And it worked. I transformed from an average student to an "A" student and from an average job earner to a top sales earner. Ironically, entering the sales world was perhaps not the best choice for a workaholic like me, as the immediate reinforcement of making more money fueled my addiction to work even further.

For most of my adult life, my identity revolved around my work. I took immense pride in my work ethic, and corporate America fully exploited individuals like me who would climb the proverbial corporate ladder tirelessly until retirement. Stepping into the entrepreneurial track was no different. As business owners, workaholics like me would keep working IN the business until it failed. And even when I started to break away from this mindset, I found myself replacing one relinquished task with another.

But then came the wake-up call: the diagnosis of cancer. It shook me to my core, and suddenly, I realized there was more to life than work and accomplishments. It ignited a burning desire for balance, fulfillment, and true happiness.

Determined to change, I embarked on a journey of self-discovery. I delved into my passions and interests beyond the confines of business. I embraced hobbies that brought me joy and reconnected with my inner self. I prioritized quality time with loved ones, nurturing the relationships I had neglected in my relentless pursuit of success.

Slowly but surely, I learned to delegate tasks and trust capable individuals to handle them. I discovered the power of teamwork and collaboration, understanding that by relinquishing control, I could achieve more together than I could alone.

As I let go of the need to micromanage every aspect of my business, I developed a newfound sense of freedom and creativity. I shifted my focus from working IN the business to working ON the business. I strategically planned and implemented long-term goals, fostering growth and innovation.

Surprisingly, my business thrived even more as I started to find balance and prioritize my well-being. Empowered by a supportive team, I witnessed the magic that happens when talented individuals come together for a common purpose. And as my business flourished, I rediscovered my own worth beyond work. Cancer forced me to confront my deeply ingrained beliefs and unhealthy work habits, but it also allowed me to rebuild a fulfilling, purposeful, and joyful life.

Chapter 14

Lifestyles Unlimited Multifamily Mentor

My real estate journey began during a challenging period in my life. I had lost my recruiting business, which meant losing a source of income, my sense of identity, and the support system I had built. However, as they say, when one door closes, another one opens. Little did I know that this new door would lead me to a remarkable community within the real estate industry.

Helping Others

Initially, what drew me to Lifestyles Unlimited was the business aspect of real estate. I was not familiar with the company's philosophy or its founder. However, the close-knit community within Lifestyles Unlimited surprised me the most and brought me immense joy over the years. It is a community of like-minded families, all sharing a common goal—to break free from the rat race of corporate America. These families possess the courage to challenge deeply ingrained beliefs that have hindered their financial progress. They are eager to help one another succeed through real estate investing. Lifestyles Unlimited has created an entire support system that is instrumental in guiding families through the intricate roadmap of real estate investing. I am grateful to be a part of this greater family of real estate investors.

Seven years ago, Del, the founder of Lifestyles Unlimited, approached me with an offer to become a multifamily mentor for his company. Without hesitation, I accepted the opportunity. Surprisingly, some of my friends questioned my decision, as they viewed it as me becoming an employee with an office—something that went against the very reason many joined Lifestyles Unlimited: to break away from the corporate world. However, from my perspective, I was honored to join an incredible team that had already helped thousands of families achieve financial freedom through real estate. Above all, this role perfectly aligned with my new mission in life post-cancer: to make a significant impact by empowering others.

Over the years, as Del expanded his company globally, he added more team members to support the growing community of over 50,000 members within Lifestyles Unlimited. The core mentoring and consulting groups, both for multifamily and single family, have an abundance of real estate experience. Gratitude is a common thread that runs through the entire organization.

"You can have everything in life you want if you will just help enough other people get what they want." –Zig Ziglar

One of the key factors contributing to the company's success is its one-on-one mentoring program. I experienced the value of this program as I navigated the complexities of the real estate world. Mentors provided step-by-step guidance through various stages, such as property locating, evaluating, negotiating, financing, closing, rehabbing, leasing, and property management. Most new members have little to no real estate experience, and even those with real estate experience often require some form of retraining. Now, I have the privilege of paying it forward and helping other members achieve financial independence by following Del's proven roadmap. Seeing members reach their financial goals and knowing I played a part in their success is an incredibly satisfying experience.

A significant portion of my mentoring is dedicated to assisting members in evaluating deals. We conduct thorough reviews using a proprietary system to analyze the data provided by sellers. Additionally, we consider all the intangible details surrounding the deal to paint a more complete picture. Through helping others, I have gained a wealth of knowledge and developed an extensive understanding of submarkets, which has proven invaluable in making my own buying decisions.

My mentoring involvement extends throughout the entire acquisition timeline, including pre-acquisition and post-closure matters. Our mentoring and consulting teams collaborate closely, constantly striving to expand our knowledge base. This collective effort enables us to deliver optimal solutions to our members.

Weekly Events

The Lifestyles Unlimited member calendar is packed with weekly events conveniently offered online and in person. My favorites among these events are the monthly education and acquisition road trips. The education road trips provide us with an immersive experience as we spend an entire day delving into the intricacies of another member's property.

The day kicks off with a formal PowerPoint presentation, followed by an in-person visit to the property in the afternoon. During these sessions, the presenting member candidly shares their challenges during the acquisition process and the strategies they employed to overcome them. They generously divulge their leasing, marketing, and operational best practices, allowing us to discover something new and valuable every time.

On the other hand, the acquisition road trips take us to explore 4 or 5 active multifamily properties currently on the market. The Lifestyles realty team provides a comprehensive overview of these properties, and members are encouraged to ask plenty of questions.

During one of these acquisition road trips, I found my first apartment—a true testament to the value of these excursions.

For newcomers, the case study night is the most beneficial event. This monthly gathering is open to the public and has been a tradition for the past thirty years. During these sessions, up to three families share their remarkable real estate journeys, with two focusing on the single-family side and one on the multifamily side. The case study nights now occur 2 or 3 times a month in various cities, offering a unique opportunity to hear authentic stories from real people about their experiences in real estate. It's an invaluable chance to gain firsthand insights and learn from the real successes and challenges of others.

Lifestyle Unlimited's expo is also open to the public. This annual event is the world's largest in-person gathering of successful real estate investors. The highlight of the event is Del's captivating keynote speech, while a close runner-up is the engaging multifamily master's tour. The expo commences with a guided bus tour visiting 4 or 5 properties owned by members. This presents an exclusive opportunity to witness some of the exceptional properties recognized within the Lifestyle Unlimited community. Lifestyle Unlimited members have won local, state, and national Apartment Association Investor of the Year Awards 16 of the last 16 years! Additionally, the expo features numerous networking sessions and educational meetings spread across its duration.

The two-day seminar is a game-changing opportunity for those inspired to take the first step in their real estate venture. It provides a transformative experience, laying a solid foundation for your journey ahead. Led by seasoned experts, it offers vital knowledge and valuable networking opportunities. While available online, I recommend attending in person for a more immersive and enriching experience. It's the perfect starting point to gain confidence and make informed decisions in this thriving industry. Remember, the first step is often the hardest but can also be the most rewarding—sending you on a successful and fulfilling real estate journey.

My journey in real estate has provided me with financial opportunities and introduced me to an incredible community of like-minded individuals within Lifestyles Unlimited. The support, guidance, and education I have received from mentors and fellow members have been instrumental in my success. Today, I am proud to be part of this thriving family of real estate investors and grateful for the chance to help others achieve their financial goals while breaking free from the confines of traditional corporate America.

It's a bit ironic how I've come full circle in my professional career. For 14 years as a recruiter before transitioning into real estate, my job was to help people find employment. Today, I assist people in escaping from the very jobs they once sought.

Epilogue

I always had an entrepreneurial spirit growing up. My parents supported every new adventure I would get myself into, from mowing lawns for half my neighborhood to starting a sign-making company in middle school. While reminiscing, I found an old business card from my early teens labeled CDH Technologies, but the details of that ambitious idea had long faded from memory.

I also stumbled across an old patent I developed when trying to start a new business in my mid-twenties. My parents? Well, they were always right there, giving me that extra push. Even when I decided to transition from accounting to sales, my parents supported my decision when most others thought it was the wrong move.

Somewhere between high school and college, I lost touch with my entrepreneurial drive. Instead, I found myself gravitating towards conventional jobs, much like many other teenagers do, in pursuit of earning a steady income. My belief was that attending college would lead me to a better-paying job, but I soon faced the harsh reality that I needed to make a significant change early on in my career.

I think the entrepreneurial spirit got reignited when I transitioned to sales. Maybe that added to my success in recruiting. There is a tremendous amount of risk involved in making a career change or starting a new business. Most can't take that leap of faith.

Sometimes, we don't have a choice. If I didn't voluntarily leave my job with the large accounting firm, I would have been forced out due to the eventual bankruptcy of the firm many years later. Sometimes life forces you to change unexpectedly, like when I had to sell my staffing company. I loved my job at that time.

Tragically, this unexpected change is all too common in the modern working world. People often dedicate years of their lives to companies they love, only to be unexpectedly laid off due to economic downturns or other external factors. It is a poignant reminder that job security is an illusion, and we must always be prepared to adapt and reinvent ourselves.

The greatest risk beyond losing a job is reaching retirement age and realizing there isn't enough money to retire comfortably. This sobering reality was underscored when I saw a YouTube video of workers at a manufacturing company being informed that their pensions were no longer viable. The uncertainty and anxiety on their faces were palpable, reminding me of the importance of taking control of one's financial future.

The flawed 401k system, plagued by excessive broker fees and financial mismanagement, adds to retirement planning uncertainty. Despite diligently contributing to social security throughout our lives and following the conventional wisdom of saving for retirement, many find themselves ill-prepared for life after work.

Check out the "E*TRADE Super Bowl 2018 Commercial" on YouTube. In this captivating ad, you will see elderly men and women sing a hauntingly fitting "Day-O, Day-O" chorus, exclaiming, "I'm 85, and I want to go home," as they insert their dentures, ride their scooters, and head to work. The scene includes a fatigued lifeguard reminiscent of "Baywatch," an old fireman struggling with a water hose, and a fur-clad grandma working as a club DJ named "DJ Nanna." E*TRADE highlights the stark reality that one-third of Americans have no retirement savings and are forced to find alternative means to make ends meet. The Super Bowl ad delivers a powerful message, urging viewers to start saving for retirement now.

Unfortunately, saving is not the answer. You can't save your way to retirement. You can't save your way to wealth. Wealth is not a pile of money. Ask your financial advisor how much money you need to retire. Their answer assumes you only have a certain number of years to live and are willing to downgrade your lifestyle according to their projections. Die before your money runs out? What kind of plan is that?

The only real solution is becoming financially independent. To have the financial freedom to continue working in a job you love, start a new business venture you always dreamed about, volunteer for a charity close to your heart, or simply enjoy life more deeply. The freedom to retire on your terms. The freedom to build generational wealth.

Starting on the path toward financial independence is crucial, and there are various ways to achieve it. Real estate offers one of the best paths to financial freedom due to its tax advantages and accessibility to leverage for generating passive income. Saving is not sufficient for a comfortable retirement.

I challenge everyone to embark on their journey toward financial freedom without delay. Let's learn from the experiences of others and take action now. The time to secure our financial future is now, so let's not wait until it's too late.

Made in the USA
Coppell, TX
18 December 2023

26430048R00081